THE JOURNAL OF
CORPORATE CITIZENSHIP

Issue 33
Spring 2009

Theme Issue: **Landmarks in the History of Corporate Citizenship**

ISSN 1470-5001

THE JOURNAL OF CORPORATE CITIZENSHIP

General Editors David Cooperrider and Ronald Fry,
The Fowler Center for Sustainable Value, Weatherhead School of Management, Case Western Reserve University, USA

Regional Editors *North America:* Professor Sandra Waddock, Boston College, Carroll School of Management, USA;
Australasia: Professor David Birch, Corporate Citizenship Research Unit, Deakin University, Australia;
Asia-Pacific: Malcolm McIntosh, Asia-Pacific Centre for Sustainable Enterprise, Griffith Business School, Australia

Publisher John Stuart, Greenleaf Publishing, UK **Production Editor** Dean Bargh, Greenleaf Publishing, UK
Book Review Editor Jerry Calton, University of Hawaii, USA

CORRESPONDENCE

The Journal of Corporate Citizenship encourages response from its readers to any of the issues raised in the journal. All correspondence is welcomed and should be sent to the General Editor via Boston College, Carroll School of Management, Chestnut Hill, MA 02467, USA; edjcc@bc.edu.

Entries for the **Diary of Events** should be marked 'JCC Diary' and sent to journals@greenleaf-publishing.com.
Books to be considered for review should be marked for the attention of the Book Review Editor and sent to Jerry Calton, School of Business and Economics, University of Hawaii–Hilo, 200 W. Kawili Street, Hilo, HI 96720, USA; calton@hawaii.edu; notification should be also sent to edjcc@bc.edu.

• All articles published in *The Journal of Corporate Citizenship* are assessed by an external panel of business professionals, consultants and academics.

• *The Journal of Corporate Citizenship* is monitored by 'Political Science and Government Abstracts' and 'Sociological Abstracts'; and indexed in the Thomson Gale Business and Company Resource Center.

SUBSCRIPTION RATES

The Journal of Corporate Citizenship is a quarterly journal, appearing in Spring, Summer, Autumn and Winter of each year. Subscription rates for organisations are £150.00 sterling/US$250.00 for one year (four issues) and for individuals £75.00 sterling/US$125.00. Cheques should be made payable to Greenleaf Publishing and sent to:

The Journal of Corporate Citizenship
Greenleaf Publishing Ltd, Aizlewood Business Centre, Aizlewood's Mill, Nursery Street, Sheffield S3 8GG, UK
Tel: +44 (0)114 282 3475 Fax: +44 (0)114 282 3476 Email: journals@greenleaf-publishing.com.
Or order from our website: www.greenleaf-publishing.com.

ADVERTISING

The Journal of Corporate Citizenship will accept a strictly limited amount of display advertising in future issues. It will also be possible to book inserts. Suitable material for promotion includes publications, conferences and consulting services. For details on rates and availability, please email journals@greenleaf-publishing.com.

BOSTON COLLEGE
CARROLL SCHOOL OF MANAGEMENT
Center for Corporate Citizenship

The Center for Corporate Citizenship at Boston College is the editorial and administrative home of *The Journal of Corporate Citizenship*. The Center's mission is to provide leadership in establishing corporate citizenship as a business essential, so all companies act as economic and social assets by integrating social interests with other core business objectives. The Center provides research, executive education, consultation and convenings on issues of corporate citizenship. For more information, visit www.bc.edu/corporatecitizenship.

FSC
Mixed Sources
Product group from well-managed forests and other controlled sources
Cert no. SGS-COC-2953
www.fsc.org
© 1996 Forest Stewardship Council

Printed and bound by CPI Group (UK) Ltd, Croydon, CR0 4YY

A Journal That Makes a Difference

David Cooperrider and Ronald Fry
The Fowler Center for Sustainable Value,
Weatherhead School of Management, Case Western Reserve University, USA

Announcing the tenureship as General Editors of David Cooperrider and Ronald Fry, who will take over from Malcolm McIntosh

IN HER SCHOLARLY ANALYSIS OF THE corporate citizenship movement, Sandra Waddock celebrates and documents the lives of *The Difference Makers*—the courageous leading-edge innovators who, starting largely in the last decades of the 20th century and early part of the 21st, created the emerging infrastructures aimed at advancing corporate citizenship, accountability and transparency. 'It is not often that we have the opportunity to hear from the founders and early pioneers of a social movement about how it grew and evolved,' says Sandra. But that is exactly what she goes on to do in her well-researched and timely book.

As the story unfolds, one of the pioneering figures is Malcolm McIntosh—the founder and first general editor of this, the *Journal of Corporate Citizenship*. Of course, Sandra's account of the creation of the journal and its widespread impact focuses on the journal's mission, its growth and its content. But it also speaks to the personal motivations and passions behind the corporate citizenship movement. Sandra's interview with Malcolm gives us a glimpse of what matters most, and why he worked so tirelessly on behalf of *JCC*:

> It's most definitely about seeing the planet as one space. It's about connecting economic, social and

environmental issues and impact and performance around the idea that we share one planetary space connected back to the human world of people, making the world a peaceful and socially just place for everybody. That's absolutely fundamental.

With this edition of the journal we want to introduce ourselves and extend our deepest appreciation for Malcolm's special leadership and his two tenures of editorship of the *JCC*. At the same time we would like to acknowledge the sterling work of both Sandra Waddock and David Birch, who both served as general editor for a two-year term, and helped it to continue to develop and grow. As we now step into the role, we want to say this to Malcolm: the *JCC* will continue to focus centrally not only on its mission of integrating theory about corporate citizenship with management practice, but it will carry forward the spirit of your work. Like you, our knowledge-interest is in 'making the world a peaceful and socially just place for everybody' and 'seeing the planet as one space'.

In this brief editorial, therefore, we wish not only to reaffirm the enduring purpose and aim of this journal but also to share several reflections on our special moment in history—and a sense of an inflection point, both for the corporate citizenship domain as well as this vital and dynamic journal.

Extraordinary times require more than ordinary journals

When judged against the needs of our times—the worst worldwide economic recession since the 1930s, the public's plummeting trust in business, deep conceptual and practical questions about responsible capitalism, as well the mounting severity of global climate change issues, poverty, the oil endgame, soaring unemployment, and many other connected complexities—it's clear that the mission of the JCC is not only relevant but it's increasingly at the centre of a huge conversation that matters. Ours *is* an extraordinary time and extraordinary times require more than ordinary conversations. Extraordinary times require penetrating insight, the creative framing of powerful questions and field-shaping forums for the exchange of informed new possibilities for bridging theory and practice. When we were asked to take on the task of editing this journal we were attracted primarily by two things: (1) the JCC aims to be the premier journal to publish articles on corporate citizenship that accomplish the integration of theory and managerial practice, and (2) the vision that 'we want the journal to be read *as much by executives* leading corporate citizenship as it is by academics seeking sound research and scholarship'.

Obviously, this is a tall order but it strikes us that this aim is more critical than ever. Speaking at the most recent World Economic Forum, Klaus Schwab argued that we are now in the midst of a 'transformational crisis' the likes of which will challenge every executive, where leaders in every sphere need to 'first help manage the crisis and second to shape the post-crisis world'. For purposes here we can build on this thought and amplify the very real questions of relevance we hope permeates every page of this journal: *How might the theories, practices and values of corporate citizenship more powerfully than ever before help managers navigate their organisations during these destabilised times?* And, *How might the lens of corporate citizenship help all of us shape the post-crisis world—including questions related to the fundamental purpose of the firm as well as solution-focused scenarios, future images, and visions of the sustainable enterprise economy of the future?*

High-priority questions of 'how'

Our own interest in corporate citizenship mushroomed in 2004 when we were asked by UN Secretary-General Kofi Annan and Georg Kell of the Global Compact to help design and facilitate the Leaders Summit at the UN. It was the largest multi-stakeholder meeting of its kind ever held at the UN and it catalysed a huge period of growth for the Global Compact. At the time the Global Compact was comprised of some 1,500 companies. By the next meeting—the Leaders Summit in Geneva Switzerland in 2007— there were more than 5,000 corporations, from Unilever to the Coca-Cola Company and from Tata Industries to Royal Dutch Shell. Likewise, the discourse on corporate citizenship, we observed, was spreading in viral fashion everywhere, moving from the margins to mainstream, and from the periphery of CEO work to the heart of strategy. Scholars introduced the language of 'next-generation citizenship' (Googins *et al.* 2007) tracing the movement from forms of ethical compliance and disclosure to strategic philanthropy, and from sustainability's triple-bottom-line focus on 'doing less harm' to a new kind of revolutionary renewal: that is, harnessing the power of markets and strengths of good enterprise to build a better society and enrich our ecosystems (see Bright *et al.* 2007).

Can we really say that the field of corporate citizenship is at an inflection point?

Again we would like to draw on our own experience and share the observation that we are indeed quickly moving into a phase where a subtle yet tectonic shift is happening. It's a moment not unlike the launch of the human genome project. It's a moment not unlike the time when the world decided to eradicate smallpox from the planet. In each of these cases, two things were happening. There was an unusually widespread and powerful vision of the 'what' (for example, 'to eradicate smallpox from the planet' or 'to identify all the 20,000–25,000 genes in human DNA and determine the sequences of the 3 billion chemical base pairs that make up human DNA') which enabled a huge shift in attention to the 'how'. Might it be that we are witnessing a similar phenomenon in the corporate citizenship movement? Might it be that the central question is shifting from the 'why' and the 'what' to 'how'?

While it is beyond the scope of this editorial to trace it adequately, we have come to believe that there is an unprecedented and increasingly shared global vision around corporate citizenship, one that is uncoordinated but emerging everywhere. In our research and at our Global Forum for *Business as an Agent of World Benefit,* we have asked over 5,000 CEOs and civil-society leaders to step beyond today's innovations and to imagine their desired 2020 future in economic, social and ecological terms (Cooperrider 2008). What we see is a remarkably clear and consistent set of responses. Envisioned is a sustainable enterprise economy and a world that:

▶ Has created a bright-green restorative economy that purifies the air we breathe

▶ Has eliminated waste and toxic by-products

▶ Has eradicated extreme poverty and preventable disease

▶ Is powered through renewable energy innovations

▶ Has made empowered prosperity accessible to everyone in the world

▶ Is supported by positive market incentives aligned with the long-term social good

▶ Has eliminated 'perverse incentives' that work against not just society but business itself

▶ Has inspired a next-generation corporate citizenship movement, which in turn has united sustainable design and business strategy into a positive race to the top

▶ Is a globally inclusive system that respects and replenishes the health of people, diverse communities, and the wealth of nature

▶ Has built its economy on a network of institutions that are trusted to elevate, magnify and refract our highest human strengths into the world

In each of our seminars and multi-stakeholder dialogues we now ask senior executives, MBA students and civil-society leaders to reflect on and improve this 2020 scenario. Invariably, people spontaneously shift their attention from the question of 'What do we want?' to 'How do we do it? How do we turn the social and global issues of our day into opportunities to create sustainable value?'

In our view this question—especially as we see it emerging as the high-priority question of business executives and the kinds of practising managers and leaders reading *this* journal—is a new emphasis. And it is a provocative one. It suggests that adopting sustainable citizenship practice is not simply an ethical obligation for businesses—it's a contemporary differentiator, a foundation for success. It promises to lead business to surprising new discoveries, stronger performance and greater significance to their owners, their members and to society.

As we move into the task of serving as editors for this great journal, we have been asked to share our point of view. What is that point of view? Put most simply, it is that *corporate citizenship is on the eve of its most important pragmatic era, and that sus-*

tainability is truly emerging as the business opportunity of the 21st century. It is an innovation engine. And it is a lens that will dominate the management agenda for the next thirty or more years. Even more important, the outcomes will define the next episode in stakeholder capitalism and ultimately will determine the well-being of our imperilled planet.

David Cooperrider's interests include the theory and practice of Appreciative Inquiry (AI) as applied to corporate strategy, change leadership and positive organisational scholarship. In addition, David is pioneering new horizons in the AI Summit method—a large-group and network-based approach—for advancing business innovation and creative design. David's most recent passion is an inquiry into 'Business as an Agent of World Benefit', where he believes that sustainable design has become the biggest business opportunity of the 21st century. David has published 14 books, authored over 50 articles, and has received numerous awards.

 David.Cooperrider@case.edu

References

Bright, David, Ron Fry and David Cooperrider (2007) 'Transformative Innovations for the Mutual Benefit of Business, Society and the Environment', in B. Googins, P. Mirvis and S. Rochlin (eds.), *Beyond Good Company* (New York: Palgrave Macmillan).

Cooperrider, David (2008) 'Sustainable Innovation', *Biz Ed*, July/August 2008: 32-38.

Googins, B., P. Mirvis and S. Rochlin (eds.) (2007) *Beyond Good Company* (New York: Palgrave Macmillan).

Waddock, S. (2008) *The Difference Makers: How Social and Institutional Entrepreneurs Created the Corporate Responsibility Movement* (Sheffield, UK: Greenleaf Publishing; www.greenleaf-publishing.com/differencemakers).

Ronald Fry's research interests focus on the factors and dynamics that foster system-wide, positive change. As a co-creator of the Appreciative Inquiry theory and method, he works with groups, organisations and institutions around the world to increase their cooperative capacity in order to engage the whole system in strategic thinking, planning and change. Through his research, he continues to develop insights on large-group dynamics, appreciative leadership, multi-stakeholder strategic planning, and business as an agent for world benefit.

 Ronald.Fry@case.edu

Editorial

Issue 33 *Spring 2009*

Malcolm McIntosh

Applied Research Centre in Human Security (ARCHS)
Coventry University, UK

Landmarks in the history of corporate citizenship: 'a slippery slope'

LADIES AND GENTLEMEN, THE company has had another excellent year. Profits have again been below those of our major competitors as a result of our heavy investment in research and development and in enhancing the skills of our workforce at all levels. But it is precisely these elements which, though reducing our immediate profits, have led to market confidence in our reputation and long-term strength—a confidence reflected in our share price which has consistently outperformed our chief rivals.[1]

This quote comes from an after-dinner speech made by Sir Geoffrey Chandler in 1999 at a corporate citizenship conference at Warwick Business School in the UK and close to the birth of the *Journal of Corporate Citizenship*. His speech was as if he were addressing the annual general meeting of X plc in May 2005, six years on. Today, ten years on, in the midst of a major global discussion concerning the future of capitalism, his words could not have been more prescient. There is now an annual

Sir Geoffrey Chandler memorial lecture in London on business and human rights to celebrate his pioneering work on Shell's business principles and also his inspiration in setting up Amnesty International's business and human rights group which he chaired from 1999 to 2007, when it was disbanded on the grounds that its 'pioneering work had been completed'. In this edition Sir Geoffrey, who remains a constantly incisively analytical and critical friend of business, writes of the history of that group and its travails and progress in 'The Amnesty International UK Business Group: Putting Human Rights on the Corporate Agenda'. I wonder if, in the light of the growth of state-owned enterprises in emerging economies and the nationalisation of many banks around the world, we can provoke him to think now in 2009 about 'the privatisation of the world economy' that took place under Reagan and Thatcher and the rejuvenation of the state as a necessary provider of social stability in the face of the market's inability to self-correct? Alan Greenspan has told us that the 30-year experiment in increasing mar-

---

1 G. Chandler, 'Annual General Meeting of X plc, May 2005: The Chairman's Speech—A Vision', in M. McIntosh (ed.), *Visions of Ethical Business 1* (London: FT Management/PricewaterhouseCoopers/CEP, 1999).

ket self-regulation has failed, and Jack Welch has told us that a sole focus on shareholder value was 'the dumbest idea', so perhaps now we can get back to intelligently redesigning global capitalism and embedding CSR in incorporation procedures. As John Ruggie did not say, 'How about embedded corporate citizenship?'

This is not a definitive history of corporate citizenship but for anyone interested in the who, what, why and how of this subject there are some very significant papers which may become definitive for scholars and reflective practitioners. Just as many people cannot imagine a world without mobile telephony and the Internet, and seem not to care or wonder how we got here, so too it is forgotten that much that is now taken for granted in terms of corporate reporting and accountability has been, and still is, the result of a hard struggle. As Chandler reflects, in 1992, when the Amnesty International Business Group asked UK-based TNCs (transnational corporations) to comment on the role of business in human rights, the Chairman of BP replied: 'I am afraid you are asking me stand at the top of a very slippery slope.'

Has the 'slippery slope' become an avalanche? Ralf Barkemeyer and colleagues write in 'What the Papers Say: Trends in Sustainability' that some terminology is now mainstream—'sustainable development' and 'corporate social responsibility', for example—while 'corporate citizenship' and 'corporate sustainability' are not common. Their analysis looked at 20.5 million articles in 340,000 papers in 39 countries in many languages from 1990 to 2008. This is a very useful piece of analysis for this edition on landmarks which now needs to be built on to see whether the continual use of these terms increases their understanding and application!

Is corporate responsibility a social movement? Many, including this editor, would argue that it is and that as it gathers momentum it becomes a much wider social movement of concerned global citizens whose interest is in broadly humanising the globalisation process so that the pillars of social and environmental practice are as well placed and sturdy as the pillars of commerce. As we saw in 2008, when the pillars made of cash collapse it brings down the whole temple and ruins the lives of millions of people going about the daily business of surviving, regenerating, sharing and caring. The human security agenda of 'freedom from want and freedom from fear' is surely at the heart of the corporate responsibility movement.

In this edition Sandra Waddock recognises a range of Western social activists who have driven corporate social responsibility onto the mainstream agenda, as witnessed by Barkemeyer *et al.* Her list of 'difference makers' is not definitive (for instance, it does not include Sir Geoffrey Chandler or Oded Grajew, Founder and President of the Ethos Institute in Brazil) but it is immensely useful for anyone wanting to understand how individuals make a crowd move—as is her book, *The Difference Makers*, on the same subject.[2]

It is interesting that the recent *Oxford Handbook of Corporate Social Responsibility* remains largely silent on the 24 'difference makers' (Waddock's 23 plus her!) and only makes one passing reference to as seminal a figure as John Elkington and the 'triple bottom line'; so what sort of handbook is it, or is it the case that the 'social movement' is not recognised by academic theorists detached from the reality of modern life on which they belatedly feed? Also, the *Oxford Handbook* refers to Chandler, A.D. (1962) but not Chandler, G. at all—a strange omission given that Chandler, G. wrote Shell's General Business Principles in 1967 and later led the UK Amnesty International Business Group for many years.

Let's mention some of Waddock's list of social activists as is appropriate in an issue of *JCC* on (recent) landmarks: Alice Tepper Marlin, Steve Lydenberg, John Elkington,

---

2 S. Waddock, *The Difference Makers: How Social and Institutional Entrepreneurs Created the Corporate Responsibility Movement* (Greenleaf Publishing, 2008; www.greenleaf-publishing.com/differencemakers).

Simon Zadek, John Ruggie and Georg Kell, Bob Massie, Allen White, Steve Waddell, Jane Nelson and Marjorie Kelly. *JCC* has published almost all of these people in previous editions and in this edition Steve Lydenberg, Allen White and Marjorie Kelly appear.

In 'From Corporate Responsibility to Corporate Design: Rethinking the Purpose of the Corporation' Allen White and Marjorie Kelly say that CSR (corporate social responsibility) was conceived just two decades ago, perhaps forgetting Robert Owen, the Quaker companies of many, many decades ago and Tata of India who go way back. They argue that the dominant ethos of the modern company 'retains a focus on short-term benefit to "owners", regardless of how remote, passive or transient they may be' and they claim that the various new initiatives on corporate conduct, including the UN Global Compact, fail to address the issue of 'purpose'. They call for corporate redesign, as they set out their model of Corporation 20/20, as corporations are currently failing to serve the needs of modern society.

Moving to the future, and building on the past, three papers in this edition take the debate further. In 'Mainstream or Daydream: The Future for Responsible Investing' Steve Lydenberg and Graham Sinclair make reference to the mainstreaming of the CSR discourse in the same vein as Ralf Barkemeyer and colleagues. Lydenberg points out that corporate executives who make reference to CSR are no longer thought of as eccentric but are still bound and obsessed by short-termism. The key is in their conclusion: 'The promise [ESG and the CSR movement offer] is a means of harnessing the creative powers of for-profit corporations in ways that complement, not undercut, government's ability to create public goods'.

According to Rory Sullivan and Stephanie Pfeifer the EU Emission Trading Scheme is one of the 'critical landmarks in the history of corporate responsibility' because it forces investors to turn their attention from the very short term to the immediate danger and long-term absolute calamity of climate change. They argue in 'Moving the Capital Markets' that this mechanism is driving change but that there are three 'substantial barriers': short-term interests still beating long-term focus for attention; a lack of policy certainty by governments so that business is unclear about future trends; and inadequate corporate disclosure hampering the real assessment of risk and opportunity.

Finally, a case study about the future, in a contentious area for the reflective practitioners and scholars who read *JCC*, on HP, the IT industry and BoP (bottom of the pyramid). The marketisation of the poorest in our communities is either one of the greatest gifts of the market to humankind or the most appalling manipulation of the most vulnerable people on Earth, according to which way you think about the 'bottom of the pyramid' hypothesis. The arguments seem to be around whether BoP empowers or enslaves those that it captures. It may be that an e-Inclusion initiative such as that described by Anke Schwittay in 'Taking Prahalad High-Tech' empowers and delivers social mobility in a way that micro-finance and repackaging soap sometimes may not.

But, as the papers in this special edition of the *Journal of Corporate Citizenship* attest, there are many in boardrooms who now know that 'the slippery slope' can lead (to paraphrase Sir Geoffrey Chandler) to market confidence in reputation and long-term strength—a confidence reflected in the share price which can out-perform rivals. Now we need again to address the issue of 'the role, scope and purpose' of the company in society.

It has been postulated that 'CSR is dead'. In one sense this is true because many of those banks awarded good corporate citizenship prizes over the last ten years and more have proved to be lacking in any principles other than greed and fraud. On the other hand, much of what the corporate citizenship movement has been arguing has come true: that greater accountability and transparency is needed, particularly when trust evaporates. But emerging is a wholly new agenda based on the fourth revolution that is sustainability. After the revolutions of agriculture, industrialisation and information comes the revolution that may enable humans to continue to live on planet Earth. This means all individuals and organs of society adapting to the new sustainable enterprise economy. We have been here for millions of years but in just 200 years we have very successfully conquered the planet and in so doing challenged our own survival. The new agenda for corporate citizenship is the same for individuals and governments: how shall we all live on one planet? All our systems need to be geared to cutting population, to being energy-efficient, to conserving water, and to building safe, fair communities. We know enough now about social democracy, that equal societies are also less violent, more socially cohesive and have lower levels of mental illness. The Scandinavians, Japan, New Zealand and to some extent Australia have won the battle of ideas—if they can curb their energy use. As John Maynard Keynes said in 1933, we now need to focus on well-being growth, not just economic growth.

Finally, I am absolutely delighted that for the next three years David Cooperrider and Ron Fry will be the new General Editors of the *Journal of Corporate Citizenship*. With their backgrounds in appreciative inquiry and focus on business as an agent for world benefit, they will bring a fresh eye and new energy (efficiently we hope!) to the journal, which, like the UN Global Compact, will celebrate its tenth birthday in 2010.

Malcolm McIntosh
March 2009

Malcolm McIntosh PhD MA Bed FRSA is Professor of Sustainable Enterprise and Director of the Asia-Pacific Centre for Sustainable Enterprise at Griffith Business School, Griffith University, Brisbane, Queensland, Australia. He is also Visiting Professor in Human Security and Sustainable Enterprise at Coventry University, England; Visiting Professor in the Department for Civil Engineering at Bristol University, England; and Professor Extraordinaire at the Sustainability Institute at Stellenbosch University in South Africa. He was the Founding Editor of the *Journal of Corporate Citizenship* in 2000. Forthcoming books are *The Next Great Transformation: SEE Change— The New Sustainable Enterprise Economy* with Sandra Waddock and Georg Kell (Greenleaf Publishing, 2010); *The Handbook on Human Security*, co-edited with Mary Martin, LSE, and Alan Hunter, Coventry University (2010); and *Human Security and Sustainable Enterprise* (2011).

 malcolm.mcintosh@btinternet.com

World Review

October–December 2008

A synopsis of the key strategic developments in corporate responsibility around the globe over the last quarter

Jem Bendell

Adjunct Associate Professor, Griffith Business School, Australia

Chew Ng

Professor of Accounting Griffith Business School, Australia

Niaz Alam

Board Member, London Pensions Fund Authority/Senior Associate, Lifeworth

Looking East

AS 2008 DREW TO A CLOSE, SOME OF THE long-term implications of the financial crisis were beginning to be seen. The shift of economic power from the West to 'the rest', which had been chronicled or predicted for some time, appeared now to be inevitable, as Western governments took on huge debts to bail out their struggling banks and companies, and stimulate their economies with public spending. This has implications for the future terrain of corporate social responsibility (CSR) issues, concepts and practice. In this review of the final quarter of 2008, we examine some of dimensions to the underlying shifts in economic power and their implications for corporate citizenship. These shifts include the growing importance of Islamic finance and of state-owned funds as investors and owners of companies worldwide, and the increasing initiatives on corporate responsibility across Asia.

Islamic finance

IN NOVEMBER 2008, THE US TREASURY Department announced that it would convene an 'Islamic Finance 101' Forum to teach Islamic Finance to US banking regulatory agencies, Congress and other parts of the executive branch in Washington, DC.[1] Collaborating with the Harvard Uni-

---

1 Chelsea Schilling, 'US Treasury teaches 'Islamic Finance 101': advisers, scholars to promote controversial Shariah funding', *World Net Daily*, 5 November 2008; www.worldnetdaily.com/index.php?fa=PAGE.view&pageId=80003.

versity's Islamic Finance Project, the purpose of this Forum is 'to help inform the policy community about Islamic financial services which are an increasingly important part of the global financial industry'.[2]

Islamic finance is a banking system that is characterised by five principles of Shari'ah or Islamic Law. These include: prohibition of interest (*riba*), prohibition of uncertainty and excessive speculation (*gharar*), prohibition of certain economic activities (including the consumption of alcohol and tobacco, gambling and pornography), share of profits or losses (*musharakah*), and use of asset-based financing (*murabaha*).[3] Islamic finance is concentrated in the Middle East and South-East Asia (predominately Indonesia and Malaysia) but is spreading into North Africa and Europe. It is regulated by the Islamic Financial Services Board (IFSB), an international standard-setting body which 'promotes and enhances the soundness and stability of the Islamic financial services industry by issuing global prudential standards and guiding principles for the industry'.[4] In 2008 the spread of Islamic finance in Western economies was highlighted when Dublin-based maritime communications group Blue Ocean Wireless secured access to debt funding of $25 million (€17 million) from Bank of London and The Middle East plc (BLME), a Shari'ah-compliant wholesale bank based in the City of London representing what 'is thought to be the first time that an Irish company has availed of Islamic finance'[5]

Islamic finance accounts for approximately US$700 billion of assets and is growing at 10–30% annually, according to

FRENCH FINANCE MINISTER
CHRISTINE LAGARDE: WOOING
ISLAMIC BANKS

Moody's Investors Service. Wall Street now offers an Islamic mutual fund and an Islamic index. The importance of the Islamic finance principles has been accepted by the UK Financial Services Authority,[6] the World Bank and the International Monetary Fund. In December 2008, the Associated Press reported that France became the latest country to woo Islamic banks.[7] Finance minister Ms Christine Lagarde, who believes that Western financial institutions could learn a thing or two from Islamic finance, promised to make necessary adjustments to the French regulatory framework so that Paris could become a major marketplace in Islamic finance.

The turmoil in global financial markets since mid-2008 has raised serious questions about prudential lending and borrowing practices, risk management and corporate governance.[8] Added to these are

---

2 ifptest.law.harvard.edu/ifphtml

3 See M. Iqbal and D.T. Llewellyn, *Islamic Banking and Finance: New Perspectives on Profit-sharing and Risk* (Cheltenham, UK: Edward Elgar, 2002).

4 www.ifsb.org

5 Ciarán Hancock, '$25m funding for Blue Ocean', *Irish Times*, 25 September 2008; www.irishtimes.com/newspaper/finance/2008/0925/1222207743548.html.

6 See the FSA white paper *Islamic Finance in the UK: Regulation and Challenges*; www.fsa.gov.uk/pubs/other/islamic_finance.pdf.

7 See Emma Vandore, 'Crisis widens appeal of Islamic finance' (24 December 2008): www.thefreelibrary.com/Crisis+widens+appeal+of+Islamic+finance-a01611751048.

8 S.J. Liebowitz, 'Anatomy of a Train Wreck: Causes of the Mortgage Meltdown', Independent Institute, 2008; www.independent.org/publications/policy_reports/detail.asp?type=full&id=30.

two behavioural problems: greed and fear.[9] The Secretary General of the Franco-Arab Chamber of Commerce, Dr Saleh Al Tayar, claimed that the €4.9 billion loss suffered by Société Générale SA as a result of Jerome Kerviel's unauthorised trading could not have happened in an Islamic financial institution.[10] And Mohammed Awan maintains that the global financial crisis 'would not have occurred if Islamic principles were applied in international financial markets'.[11] This is because, under Shari'ah principles, one cannot 'sell debt against debt'. In turn, greed leads to sale of dubiously rated collateralised debts. A further reason advanced is that Islamic finance principles require deals to be based on tangible assets that require tight controls over debt levels.

In relation to *sukuk* (bond) issues, Shari'ah rules require bondholders to be undivided partners in the underlying asset(s) that are being financed. Accordingly, the effect on Islamic financial institutions has been muted as *sukuk* instruments are generally held to maturity.[12] Thus, narrow yield spreads provide less occasion for speculation in secondary markets. Some proponents argue there is minimal probability of default with *sukuks* since issuers are able to meet payment obligations.[13]

Moody's in its November 2008 report shows that Islamic financial institutions have been quite resilient in the current global financial crisis. As an interesting aside, no Islamic bank has acknowledged investing in Bernard Madoff's US$50 billion fraudulent Ponzi scheme.[14] The resilience of Islamic finance is summarised by Zarina Anwar[15] as follows:

> The development of Islamic finance in general is also important from the perspective of financial stability . . . The Shariah-based approach contains in-built checks and balances through risk- and profit-sharing structures. More critically, it demands a high level of disclosure and transparency in the financial system which is consistent with the principles of sound securities regulation as well as in compliance with Shariah requirements. This is not to say that Islamic asset markets have not been affected by the current turmoil. Indeed it has, and the value of Shariah compliant equities has declined in tandem with that of global equities. But it has been shown that Islamic finance in various segments of the market has been able to weather the storm relatively better than its conventional counterpart.

Nevertheless, the impact of an economic downturn and evaporating asset values was having an effect on Islamic financial institutions, and led to a number of events at the end of 2008 to discuss measures to mitigate those impacts. For example, on 25 October 2008, the Islamic Development ment Bank convened an urgent meeting to discuss the impact of the global financial crisis on the Islamic banking industry and agreed on policy initiatives to tackle the challenges and opportunities for the industry. In November in Kuala Lumpur, the IFSB and the Institute of International Finance (IIF) jointly organised a conference, entitled *Enhancing the Resilience and Stability of the Islamic Financial System*, to

---

9 Hersh Shefrin and Meir Statman, *Beyond Greed and Fear: Understanding Behavioral Finance and the Psychology of Investing* (Boston, MA: Harvard Business School Press, 2002).

10 See Vandore, *op. cit.*

11 Mohammad Awan, 'Islamic finance could have avoided subprime crisis', Islamic Finance Blog, 14 May 2008; islamicfinancenews.wordpress.com/2008/05/14/islamic-finance-could-have-prevented-subprime-crisis.

12 'Sukuk strikes the right chord', Islamic Finance Asia, August/September 2008; www.islamicfinanceasia.com/cover.php.

13 *Islamic Finance News Guide 2008*; www.islamicfinancenews.com/pdf/guide08.pdf.

14 See Vandore, *op. cit.*

15 Anwar, Zarina, 'Coping with the Global Financial Turmoil, Restoring Investor Confidence', 13th Malaysian Capital Market Summit 2008, Kuala Lumpur, 4 December 2008; www.sc.com.my/main.asp?pageid=375&linkid=2000&yearno=2008&mod=paper.

examine whether the Islamic financial system is strong enough to weather the crisis. The connectedness of global finance and the global economy means that, although principles may protect Islamic financial institutions from the extreme impacts of the financial crisis, they cannot be insulated entirely. This raises a question that has hitherto been avoided by the Islamic finance community: should they engage more assertively in international policy processes to promote their principles to non-Islamic governments and financial institutions, for mutual benefit? An affirmative would imply a reversal of a dominant assumption of recent centuries: that the 'West' has a version of economics that is suitable for the rest of the world, while non-Western approaches are seen as exotic, at best filling a niche, at worst being mere artefacts from pre-modern societies. That is an assumption that some non-Western communities have been complicit in maintaining, by assuming their own ways of organising are specific to their society, rather than relevant for all societies.

The rest of the world could benefit from the Islamic financial community assuming a greater role in international initiatives to achieve financial stability. That is not only because of the problems described above, but because Islamic finance recognises the deep problems associated with interest. As money enters economies as debt, being lent by banks, so interest is attached, thereby requiring organisations and people to pay back more than they originally borrow. This creates a growth imperative, as the economy must keep expanding in order that the interest is paid. That poses a problem for a world of finite resources. Interest also promotes a competitive approach to society, as people need to acquire more money than they began with, because of the interest payments. In his description of money systems, one of the originators of the euro,

Bernard Lietaer, explains how interest-money therefore necessitates increasing economic inequality.[16] Although many financial institutions would be wary of Islamic finance principles being seen as a blueprint for a new global financial system, as it would curtail many of their lucrative but risky activities, leaders of the 'real economy' could support such a view, as they would benefit from a more stable financial system. That is not to say that Islamic finance does not present areas for substantial refinement. First, the emphasis on debtors having tangible assets could restrict loans to the economically disadvantaged, such as those currently being helped through microfinance. In addition, the processes for discriminating against certain economic activities or systems of financing on the grounds of their being considered morally inappropriate would need to be refined. For instance, the *sukuk* market declined at one point in 2008 as a 'Bahrain-based group of Islamic scholars decreed . . . that most bonds ran afoul of religious rules . . . Only one that complies with the edict has been issued, pushing up borrowing costs on projects including $200 billion of real-estate developments in the United Arab Emirates capital'.[17] The growth of Islamic finance therefore raises challenging questions about the accountability of those who have greater power in interpreting religious texts and their contemporary spiritual implications. This highlights how an 'Eastern turn' in economic power is likely to present a range of novel questions for corporate responsibility.

Sovereign wealth fund responsibility

AS THE BANKING CRISIS DEEPENED, media attention increased on the role and

16 B.A. Lietaer, *The Future of Money: Creating New Wealth, Work and a Wiser World* (Century, 2001).
17 Haris Anwar, 'Islamic bond decree cripples sukuk, imperils projects (Update 2)', Bloomberg.com, 3 September 2008; www.bloomberg.com/apps/news?pid=20601109&sid=a_Zhoq7oaPxY&refer=home.

size of sovereign wealth funds (SWFs), which played a major role in the multi-billion-dollar bailouts of Western banks such as Citigroup and UBS. Rising energy prices and trade surpluses by exporting nations enabled SWFs to grow to control assets worth an estimated $3 trillion, a figure that the Organisation for Economic Cooperation and Development (OECD) estimated could increase to around $10–12 trillion by 2012. The rise of these government-owned foreign investment funds is, the BBC notes, 'one sign of the shift in the balance of power in the world economy from Western industrialised countries to new emerging market giants like China and the oil-rich Middle East'.[18]

HUGO CHAVEZ: A POLITICAL LEADER WHO 'MIXES INVESTMENTS WITH POLITICS'

How does the emergence of SWFs relate to corporate responsibility? In at least two ways. First, as investors and owners of companies, they become relevant for assessment by firms with policies on whom they do business with. Second, as asset owners they have responsibilities to their ultimate beneficiaries, which are their national governments, and to others they affect through their investment decisions: sovereign wealth fund CSR.

The first area was highlighted when The Co-operative Bank in the UK publicly stated a policy on SWFs, based on its policies excluding business with companies connected with countries with poor human rights records. One league table (see Table 1 overleaf), of the world's 12 largest SWFs, shows that only four are from countries with democratically elected governments, although neither Russia nor Singapore was rated as fully free by Freedom House. Barry Clavin, The Co-operative Bank's ethical policies manager, explained, 'our policy precludes us from investing in an oppressive regime or in businesses and investments owned by an oppressive regime. Any business more than 20 per cent-owned by a blacklisted sovereign wealth fund will be turned down for business.'[19] Given the growth of SWF investing in Western companies, that stance may become difficult to maintain, as well as raising questions about its efficacy in either promoting social change or more effectively managing financially relevant human rights risks.

The second area of relevance for corporate citizenship is that of the SWFs' own responsibilities as private institutions—both to their beneficiaries and wider stakeholders. As the SWF assets are state-owned, we might expect them to be managed as those states see fit. The investments of SWFs have therefore raised concerns in the West that (Western) strategic assets such as banks and energy firms may end up in the hands of (unstable or unfriendly) foreign governments.[20] Concerns of stakeholders in countries receiving inward investment from SWFs therefore became more widely discussed during 2008. A McKinsey report on the topic even cited Venezuela's President Hugo Chavez as an example 'of a political leader who mixed investments with politics'[21] as an illustration of the growing calls for new rules for SWF investments.

---

18 'IMF deal on foreign wealth funds', BBC News, 3 September 2008; news.bbc.co.uk/1/hi/business/7595672.stm.

19 Patrick Hosking, 'Co-op boycotts funds over human rights', *The Times*, 21 May 2008; business.timesonline.co.uk/tol/business/industry_sectors/banking_and_finance/article3972375.ece.

20 Kevin Lim, 'IMF says voluntary code for sovereign funds by October', ArabianBusiness.com, 10 July 2008; www.arabianbusiness.com/524417-imf-says-voluntary-code-for-sovereign-funds-by-oct.

21 'OECD countries commit to open climate for Sovereign Wealth Funds', Paris, 6 June 2008; trade.ec.europa.eu/doclib/docs/2008/june/tradoc_139096.pdf.

Fund	US$ (billions)	State and Freedom House rating
Abu Dhabi Investment Council	875	UAE not free
Government Pension Fund of Norway	380	Norway free
Government of Singapore Investment Corp.	330	Singapore Partly free
Saudi Arabia—various	300	Saudi Arabia not free
Kuwait Investment Authority	250	Kuwait partly free
China Investment Corp	200	China not free
Hong Kong Monetary Authority	163	Hong Kong partly free; China not free
Temasek Holdings	159	Singapore partly free
Stabilisation Fund	157	Russia not free
Australian Future Fund	61	Australia free
Qatar Investment Authority	50	Qatar not free
Libya Arab Foreign Investment Co.	50	Libya not free

Note. This table is used to illustrate The Co-operative Bank's SWF stance; it is based on estimates that may underplay the influence of some countries via Bank investments and currency reserves (such as Japan and China) as well as excluding Western public pension funds that are regulated and potentially influenced by their governments.

Table 1 OECD ESTIMATES AND FREEDOM HOUSE HUMAN RIGHTS RATINGS, JUNE 2008
Sources: SWF Institute, IFSL estimates and Freedom House rankings; originally published in *The Times*, 21 May 2008

Traditionally, however, despite periodic press coverage about human rights abuses by some SWF regimes, both investor and investee country governments have taken a laissez-faire approach to the role of SWFs, with investee nations tending to welcome investments and SWFs tending to shy away from controversy and any appearance of interference in other states' affairs. For instance, China, Singapore and Saudi Arabia have historically downplayed the extent of their governments' potential influence on investments in the West.[22] On the other side of the SWF coin, as Western economies tend to be the major recipients of their investment funds, the OECD has argued the world economy benefits from the growth of sovereign wealth funds, 'which recycle the trade surpluses earned by oil producers and manufacturing exporters like China back into the world economy' and point out that OECD countries should be as open to investment as they have called on other countries to be.[23] The occasional high-profile protectionist stances by US lawmakers to foreign investment (for example, objecting to Dubai Ports' takeover of UK company P&O because of its US port interests on 'security grounds') have been atypical or driven by short-term political concerns. More frequently, the default position has been for governments to avoid public interference as far as possible.

This debate led to some increased transparency: for instance, by the Government of Singapore Investment Corp. (GIC), which publicly released its annual report for the first time in 2008 'to help allay Western fears that their investments are

---

22 Diana Farrell, 'The New Power Brokers', *BusinessWeek*, 15 July 2008; www.mckinsey.com/mgi/mginews/new_power_brokers.asp.
23 'IMF deal on foreign wealth funds' (*op. cit.*).

politically motivated',[24] following GIC's $18 billion investments in the struggling UBS and Citigroup.

Given the continuing concerns from recipient countries, and the potential backlash against SWF investments, an IMF-hosted working group involving 23 investing and recipient countries agreed a voluntary code to increase transparency by SWFs in order to 'promote a clearer understanding of the institutional framework, governance, and investment operations of SWF, thereby fostering trust and confidence in the international financial system'.[25] It was a challenging task, given the SWFs all have different sources of capital, different legal statuses, different mandates and different investment policies. In October the working group released the Santiago Principles—also known as the Generally Accepted Principles and Practices (GAPP). The principles cover areas such as SWFs' meeting of local recipient regulatory requirements, making public disclosures in a variety of areas, and investing on the basis of economic and risk-and-return considerations. The principles were founded on the notion of keeping politics out of the way of SWF investment, whether the politics of the recipient or investor country.

Although some questioned whether the code would really restrict political involvement in the management of the funds and thus the companies they invest in, what matters more for corporate responsibility and responsible investment is the way the code reasserts the primacy of financial value over other values, and limits fiduciary duty to solely financial considerations. Thus, SWF managers may become more accountable through procedures associated with the measurement of the financial performance of their funds, yet less accountable to the people whose savings created the funds in the first place, because their interests are assumed to be purely financial. If, as a result, managers

NORWAY'S FINANCE MINISTER KRISTIN HALVORSEN: EXCLUDING RIO TINTO ON ETHICAL GROUNDS

of large companies worldwide can access funds that are purely interested in financial returns, this may not help achieve greater corporate accountability, and could undermine the move towards more active and responsible ownership typified by the development of the UN Principles for Responsible Investment (UNPRI).

In 2008 one SWF was a member of the UNPRI. The Norwegian Government Pension Fund–Global, with an estimated US$390 billion-worth of assets, is the world's second largest SWF after the Abu Dhabi Investment Authority. It highlighted its uniquely active ethical policy by selling its US$500 million stake in Rio Tinto, a leading UK-based mining company for potentially subjecting it to 'grossly unethical conduct'. Norway's finance minister, Kristin Halvorsen, said its concerns related to Rio Tinto's joint venture with US-based Freeport McMoRan, a company excluded by the fund in 2006, for a mining operation in the Indonesian province of West Papua. In a statement on the ministry's website, she said,

> Exclusion of a company from the fund reflects our unwillingness to run an unacceptable risk of contributing to grossly unethical conduct. The council on ethics has concluded that Rio Tinto is directly involved, through its participation in the Grasberg mine in Indonesia, in

24 Kevin Lim and Saeed Azhar, 'GIC has large cash pile, sees opportunities in US', Reuters, 23 September 2008; www.reuters.com/article/ousiv/idUSTRE48M3RT20080923.
25 Lim, *op. cit.*

the severe environmental damage caused by that mining operation.[26]

The Grasberg complex is the biggest gold mine and third largest copper mine in the world. Environmental groups and local people are concerned with the environmental damage caused by dumping millions of tonnes of ore waste into the local river. Last year, a study published by the campaigning charity War on Want claimed that local people had suffered serious human rights and environmental abuses. Rio Tinto spokesman Nick Cobban expressed surprise to the *Guardian* at the Norwegian move, saying, 'Our immediate response is one of surprise and disappointment. We have an exemplary record in environmental matters—world leading, in fact—and they are given the very highest priority in everything we do.'[27] The *Guardian* also quoted Ruth Tanner, campaigns and policy director at War on Want, welcoming the decision to exclude Rio Tinto and challenging other funds to follow its lead: 'The Norwegian government has again put its money where its mouth is to ensure a real ethical investment policy. Now other pension funds should follow Norway's example.'[28]

The unprecedented level of investment transparency practised by Norway's SWF potentially makes it easy for other investors to follow suit and to leverage its global influence. Norway's SWF invests profits from oil and gas in a portfolio of around 7,000 companies around the world. The fund's ethical policy is based on applying to its investments the spirit of international agreements and ethical norms (such as ILO [International Labour Organisation] conventions) signed by the Norwegian government.

The bulk of the fund's ethical activity is in common with a growing number of public pension funds, largely based on engagement with companies in which it is invested. What sets it apart is the combination of the sheer size of its holdings and the ability and willingness of its Ethics Council (governed separately by the Ministry of Finance) to recommend shares for disinvestment. Of the 27 companies disinvested by Norway's investment programme on ethical grounds since 2005, the majority relate to governmental objections to certain types of military and nuclear weapons hardware. Boeing, Raytheon, Northrop Grumman and Lockheed are among the leading US arms companies excluded along with Britain's leading arms manufacturer BAE Systems, Thales of France and UK support services group Serco, which was removed in 2007 because of its involvement in the UK Atomic Weapons Establishment at Aldermaston.[29] The Norwegian Ethics Council has also disinvested from major companies for 'serious, systematic or gross violations of ethical norms', notably Wal-Mart for alleged complicity in breaches of international labour standards (including child labour, gender discrimination and the blocking of unionisation attempts). As the fund itself acknowledges, while disinvestment may continue to be applied in some high-profile cases, its preferred strategy remains engagement on a broad range of ethical issues.

As you may have noticed, this actively responsible approach from Norway's SWF is a form of politics: it derives from the interests of the Norwegian government in certain social and environmental principles. Therefore, its engagement in the development of the SWF code led to an interesting compromise, illustrated by the paradoxical Principle 19. It reads that 'The SWF's investment decisions should aim to maximize risk-adjusted financial returns

---

26 Terry Macalister, 'Investment: Norway offloads £500m of Rio Tinto shares over "unethical" mine stake', *The Guardian*, 10 September 2008; www.guardian.co.uk/business/2008/sep/10/riotinto. mining.
27 *Ibid.*
28 *Ibid.*
29 *Ibid.*; and Tarjei Kidd Olsen, 'Norway: oil fund finds ethical success', Global News Blog, 31 July 2008; globalnewsblog.com/wp/?p=316.

in a manner consistent with its investment policy, and based on economic and financial grounds', but then continues in a subprinciple that 'If investment decisions are subject to other than economic and financial considerations, these should be clearly set out in the investment policy and be publicly disclosed', further qualifying that 'The management of an SWF's assets should be consistent with what is generally accepted as sound asset management principles.' Principle 21 goes further in describing the nature of the shareholder activism and engagement that will be acceptable, saying, 'if an SWF chooses to exercise its ownership rights, it should do so in a manner that is consistent with its investment policy and protects the financial value of its investments'. These principles limit the exercise of social responsibility from SWFs, including Norway, to approaches that have demonstrable financial benefits. As previous World Reviews have outlined, the 'enhanced risk management' approach to responsible investment is only one approach, with some recognising how individual savers, as human beings, have interests that extend beyond the financial, whatever timeframe is applied.

The code is what one would expect from a group convened by the IMF, given its ideological bias towards traditional financial disciplines, and the fact that this code was developed to defend SWFs from Western scepticism. A much-needed dialogue would focus on what active responsible ownership can look like when being pursued by SWFs from the Gulf or Asia, rather than Scandinavia. Just because the latter have been historically more active on their concerns for people in other countries, and come from a cultural and political tradition less complicated for the West than those from the Middle or Far East, does not mean that only their form of shareholder activism should be welcomed. Without such dialogue on what are universally acceptable ways of governments, or any organisation, pursuing their full range of interests through their commercial activities, this code will soon lose legitimacy among SWF nations, and, as world power shifts, may be increasingly ignored.

For now, the code means the SWFs are tethered to the shareholder-value paradigm and thus environmental, social and governance (ESG) concerns can be forwarded only in terms of enhanced risk management. Therefore, the opportunity lies in corporate responsibility advocates seizing on Principle 22's statement that 'The SWF should have a framework that identifies, assesses, and manages the risks of its operations' and promoting a fuller understanding of ESG-related risk management.

From CSR in Asia to Asian CSR

THE SHIFT IN POWER FROM THE WEST TO the 'rest' indicates a growing role for Asian enterprise, not only within Asia itself but also in the rest of the world. Consequently, the evolution of corporate responsibility concepts, policies, practices and initiatives across the region is important worldwide. In the last quarter of 2008 a flurry of conferences confirmed the growth of corporate responsibility as a topic of business interest in the region. Despite the economic downturn, Singapore hosted a number of these events, beginning in October with the Asia Pacific Academy of Business in Society (APABIS)[30] gathering academics and business people to develop this emerging network. The following month delegates amassed at the Asian Forum on CSR,[31] which focused on giving executives a platform to promote their corporate responsibility programmes, and then at the Global Social Innovators Forum,[32] which celebrated individuals who are innovating new approaches in both

---

30 www.apabis.org
31 www.asianforumcsr.com
32 www.socialinnovatorsforum.org

business and charity, to address public challenges.

The most content-driven event of the conferencing season was the CSR Asia Summit[33] in Bangkok, which brought together innovative practitioners from different sectors, chosen by the leading specialist consultants on corporate responsibility in the region, CSR Asia. The very growth of this organisation, now with dozens of staff in five offices, is an indicator of the development of the responsible business agenda. At the summit, Leontien Plugge of the Global Reporting Initiative highlighted that Asia is now the second largest reporting region, although this is mainly due to the high rate of sustainability reporting in Japan. As some Asian governments and stock exchanges had announced during 2008 that they will introduce requirements to report on CSR and sustainability, other countries' reporting rates are set to increase.[34] To gauge the general level of CSR disclosure at present, the 'CSR Asia Business Barometer 2008' was launched at the event. This report compares the CSR disclosure of the 20 largest listed companies in Hong Kong, Malaysia, Singapore and Thailand. Commenting on the results, CSR Asia's Executive Director Erin Lyon said that 'companies listed in Hong Kong demonstrate a superior quality of CSR disclosure' although 'the majority of companies listed in each of the countries have significant room for improved disclosure'. CLP (China Light & Power) came top of their ranking. A potential concern for the United Nations' efforts in this field emerged from the study, as Ms Lyon noted that Global Compact membership had no measurable impact whatsoever on the level of disclosure of companies in the region.[35]

The discussions at these conferences give some insight into the emerging dimen-

CSR ASIA EXECUTIVE DIRECTOR ERIN LYON: 'COMPANIES LISTED IN HONG KONG DEMONSTRATE A SUPERIOR QUALITY OF CSR DISCLOSURE'

sions of Asian CSR, as a global phenomenon, rather than just CSR in Asia. First, the philosophical bases for corporate responsibility are being discussed. Kasit Piromya, the Director of International Affairs of the Democrat Party of Thailand, and the Thailand representative of the Caux Round Table, spoke at the CSR Asia Summit about a parallel between Buddhist philosophy and CSR, owing to the emphasis on stakeholder interdependence:

> Buddhist monks live according to the principle of interconnectivity with the community and the environment; they are one with their stakeholders. Similarly, every individual belongs to an organization, and ultimately to society. So every individual, while working to earn a living and enjoy the rewards, is inter-dependent on the business community and society as a whole. Along with its stakeholders business is a part of a whole and thus the need for social responsibility and good governance. In particular, large multinational corporations have a global responsibility, and not only to their financial stakeholders.[36]

33 www.csr-asia.com/summit08
34 Rikke Netterstrom, 'Sustainability reporting: it is painful, but gets easier', *CSR Asia Weekly*, Vol. 4 Week 47 (19 November 2008); www.csr-asia.com/upload/cover/703885681578.pdf.
35 'CSR Asia Business Barometer 2008: The State of CSR Disclosure in Asia'; www.csr-asia.com/upload/Barometer_Research_Brochure_2008.pdf.
36 Catherine Walter, 'Welcoming Remarks and Keynote Speeches', *CSR Asia Weekly* Vol. 4 Week 46 (12 November 2008); www.csr-asia.com/upload/cover/888330905168.pdf.

KASIT PIROMYA: A
PARALLEL BETWEEN
BUDDHIST
PHILOSOPHY AND CSR

As Buddhism is one of the many spiritual traditions in the region, there is much to be drawn on in elaborating on concepts and motives for Asian CSR.

The second dimension to the evolution of an Asian CSR is the innovation that is occurring in CSR from within the region that may have a global impact. The conference in Bangkok hosted a workshop exploring a new initiative in reporting—imPACT. This approach brings together dynamic stakeholder engagement with a new approach to communication. Developed jointly by Edelman and CSR Asia, the imPACT philosophy is based on the understanding that many companies face critical societal challenges that they can play a role in addressing through outcome-oriented partnerships. Thus, CSR actions can be mobilised around issues such as climate change, water, human rights, poverty alleviation or health, so that companies become partners in addressing public need, rather than making minor improvements on a diverse set of issues aimed to benefit corporate reputation. Emphasis is placed on shared responsibility and joint accountability with the other organisations and sectors with which a company engages.[37]

A third dimension to the evolution of Asian CSR is the growing recognition within individual Asian countries of hav-

ing the potential to play a global role. This was highlighted by the awards given out at the Global Social Innovators Forum (GSIF). The event was hosted by the Singapore-based Social Innovation Park (SIP), and focused on celebrating global leaders in social enterprise. Founder and President of SIP Penny Low said that

> SIP Fellow Awards recognize outstanding and high achieving individuals who are creating systemic change in the community that they live and work in. Role models in their own fields, these individuals are action leaders, who are shaping the future in their own way and by doing what they do best. They are the future world leaders of the globe.[38]

The Distinguished Fellow Award went to Jet Li, the Chinese actor, for his fundraising activities during 2008. One of the Fellow Awards went to Amit Wanchoo, Managing Director of Eaton Laboratories, for his work with the poor in Kashmir. In his acceptance speech Dr Wanchoo explained that 'in economically challenging times like these, social innovation remains more pertinent and relevant than ever'. He explained that 'social entrepreneurship brings together everyone's strengths to create the greatest social impact possible. I believe that collaborative innovations can help in sowing the seeds of positive change in this world for the well being of the whole humanity. We collaborate not as different sectors but as one people with one dream of a better world.'[39] In discussions with JCC, Penny Low recognised the significance of this growing international outlook: 'The SIP Fellow Award and the SIP Distinguished Fellow Award are the first Singapore-originated awards given to international recipients who excel in the field of social innovation.'

Although there is great potential for diverse approaches to emerge and impact

---

37 Mabel Wong, 'CSR Reporting through Project Partnerships: The Case of imPACT', *CSR Asia Weekly*, Vol. 4 Week 47 (19 November 2008); www.csr-asia.com/upload/cover/703885681578.pdf.

38 'Wanchoo gets SIP Fellow Award', *Rising Kashmir News*, 2008; www.risingkashmir.com/index.php?option=com_content&task=view&id=9133.

39 *Ibid.*

on the global experience of corporate responsibility, the development of CSR in Asia also poses a number of unique challenges. Currently, many Asian companies' voluntary engagement with the social and environmental performance of their business has been very influenced by the West. Therefore, at the conferences chronicled above, senior managers and government officials expressed the view that the main motivation for improved corporate responsibility is to achieve better relations with CSR-sensitive export markets. This approach can downplay or even ignore local stakeholder interests in the role and performance of business. The assumption is made that local stakeholder interests in business performance can be articulated through government, and, where that is not the case, that those stakeholder interests are not particularly valid. This view is a result of the dominant role of the state in many Asian countries and the variable, often weak, levels of civil society organising, media independence and political debate. This state of affairs may hamper the emergence of domestic CSR agendas in Asia.

Such an emergence may also be hampered by the imbalance in domestic voices involved in shaping the future of CSR. The evidence from these conferences is that the corporate responsibility debate in Asia is being influenced not by those who are directly impacted within the region, but by business leaders, government officials and high-society elites. This may be why, even now, CSR is most often construed by Asian business leaders as corporate philanthropy. This is highlighted by the fact that all of the 2008 Asian CSR awards went to philanthropic projects, bar the workplace award for Microsoft Philippines (a company that was not facing difficult workplace issues, does not have a trade union nor a systematic approach to checking what international labour standards apply to its operations). Further illustrating an emphasis on philanthropy rather than economic justice, at the GSIF most of the examples of 'social enterprise' were actually charitable activities involving some trading, such as the sale of charity-branded goods. The discussion of actions transforming core business practices on issues that have involved significant conflicts with affected stakeholders were conspicuous by their absence.

Although there are signs that at both conceptual and practical levels we are seeing the emergence of Asian CSR rather than simply more CSR in Asia, currently the majority of activities carrying the CSR tag are a mix of Western imposition and preening by local elites. If this subjugated dimension to CSR in Asia dominates practice, rather than a more organic emergence of ideas and innovations from dialogues and contestations of peoples from across the region, the loss will be both Asia's and the world's. One implication, therefore, is the need for greater awareness of the levels and nature of endogenous desire across Asia for socially progressive enterprise, and the relative roles of government, business and wider civil society in shaping and responding to that desire.

---

* Opinions expressed in this World Review are the authors' and do not necessarily reflect those of Greenleaf Publishing.

Turning Point

From Corporate Responsibility to Corporate Design

Rethinking the Purpose of the Corporation*

Marjorie Kelly and Allen L. White
Tellus Institute, USA

THESE ARE TRYING TIMES FOR CSR (corporate social responsibility). Two decades after its conception, one senses among many a kind of fatigue, impatience, even despair about the limits of CSR. A recent meta-study finds no evidence that CSR consistently yields positive returns to companies (Margolis *et al.* 2008). Another asserts that CSR is destined to always live in the shadow of issues more central to market competitiveness and that the '[perceived] business case lives on, and is always about to be proven; but it never is, nor will be' (Vogel 2008). In a similar vein, sceptics point to the inescapable reality that CSR is nothing more than smart management cloaked in the language of morality and ethics (Reich 2007).

Taken together, these perspectives yield a picture of CSR as a contingent movement, involving actions that will be undertaken only if the demands of priority stakeholders—namely investors and consumers—are concurrently met. It is time to think more systemically, beyond the boundaries of CSR, if business is to achieve the level of social contribution it is uniquely capable of making.

Design obsolescence

In historical perspective, CSR practices are but a modest diversion from the long march towards the dominance of capital interests in shaping the modern corporation. Business leaders operate today inside a corporate design of ownership and governing structures largely inherited from the 19th century. In that time, when nature offered seemingly unlimited resources, we had not yet confronted the ecological limits we face today. In that era, when labour meant interchangeable strong backs wielding hammers and picks, employee knowledge and capacity to innovate did not yet represent the foundation of competitive advantage. In that

* An earlier version of this paper was prepared for *The Summit on the Future of the Corporation*, Boston, 13–14 November 2007 (www.summit2020.org, accessed 15 January 2009). The authors gratefully acknowledge the contributions of the many Corporation 20/20 (www.corporation2020.org, accessed 15 January 2009) participants whose insights and expertise helped shape the arguments in this paper.

time of hands-on ownership by company founders and direct investors, it was impossible to imagine today's environment of dispersed and passive shareholding, where ownership shares are traded in nanoseconds.

While these elements inside and outside the corporation have changed dramatically, surprisingly little has changed in the design of corporate forms. The dominant ethos retains a focus on short-term benefit to 'owners', regardless of how remote, passive or transient they may be. Within this narrow purpose, we struggle to fit contemporary concerns.

Consider how corporate design challenges play out in the competing demands faced by corporations:

- ▶ In the wake of the financial crisis in late 2008, the US government invested US$188 billion in the nation's largest banks, in the hope that they would resume lending. But most have not done so. In the three months ending 30 November 2008, new loans to large companies actually declined by nearly 40% from the previous three months. In the absence of any mandates to increase lending—which were never made explicit—the banks have followed their traditional aim: to protect their own interests, which means hunkering down and disregarding the public good

- ▶ Companies such as Nike, Disney and New Balance have sought to create protection for workers in their overseas supply chain. Yet these companies send mixed messages. Their codes of conduct tell suppliers to run safe workplaces and pay fair wages, while their purchasing managers insist on low-cost products delivered on highly demanding schedules. Resolving this contradiction is an issue of corporate design, of how to bring social issues from the periphery to the core of company concerns

- ▶ BP's reputation as a responsible company was blemished in 2005 with the death of 15 people and injury to 180 in

an explosion at the Texas City Refinery, Texas, after the company decided to reduce costs by skimping on maintenance. The company has not resolved its central design challenge: how to structure decision-making to give priority to long-term safety instead of short-term cost-cutting aimed at increasing earnings and share price

Banks unwilling to serve the public interest despite public funding, well-intentioned but ultimately ineffective factory auditing, under-funded maintenance at an oil company: these seemingly disparate problems are symptomatic of something deeper. That something is an invisible issue—a problem that has had no name, that remains absent from the dialogue of CSR sceptics who are loud on problem definition but quiet on solutions. That issue is the design of the organisation.

A new public idea: corporate design

Corporate design is the missing business and public policy issue of the day. It is connected to countless other major issues: the working poor, the shrinking middle class, wealth concentration, the ecological crisis. We can no longer deal with these as separate and unrelated. We face today an historic moment when a fragmented, reactive approach to CSR must give way to a systemic and structural approach commensurate with the expanding impact of the modern corporation.

Corporate design is about the purpose of the firm, and about the systems and structures that give life to that purpose (Kelly and White 2007). It's about a narrow purpose inherited from the 19th century that is increasingly outmoded in the 21st century. It's about the obligations a company has to those affected by its activities. In a tangible sense, corporate design is about creating parity between social and financial considerations, both in external accountability and internal operations.

Most people assume, without explanation, that profit-making and shareholder value are the corporation's inviolable core—something akin to natural law, like gravity or thermodynamics. They are not to be subject to fundamental change, only modulated with piecemeal approaches aimed at specific harms. Contemporary CSR is simply the latest expression of this fragmented approach.

Corporate design has never been subject to the processes essential to building any governing institution, the processes by which governing frameworks have been forged in democratic nations the world over. Such processes—whether in the US, European Union, Japan or South Africa—share two commonalities. The first is a foundation of **shared principles** built through a political process, sometimes peacefully, sometimes through strife. The second is a set of **operating elements** that translate principles into institutional designs. It is time that we begin a similar kind of public process, focused on corporate design.

Principles related to corporate conduct, of course, have existed for many years. These include the OECD Guidelines for Multinational Enterprises and Principles of Corporate Governance, and the UN Global Compact Principles. Yet none of these explicitly deals with corporate purpose. Indeed, frameworks such as the Principles of Corporate Governance are largely captive to the shareholder-centric view of the corporation that lies at the root of the shortcomings we face today. Strengthening shareholder rights is, at best, an uncertain pathway to a new corporate architecture honouring multi-stakeholder rights.

We can't solve the problem of corporate design using past approaches to reform. We can't solve it by listing every possible harm or every positive contribution and then writing laws to prohibit or mandate specific corporate actions. We can't solve it by having corporations devote 1% of profits to philanthropy, or by incentivising piecemeal CSR initiatives. The inadequacy of such approaches is what makes necessary the deeper approach of corporate design (White 2006).

All those connected to corporations are caught in corporations' inadvertent design—investors and executives as much as employees and citizens. But our current choices are not immutable. They can be changed through a combination of organisational choice, legal reform and public pressure. Intentional redesign can build equitable and resilient organisations committed to long-term wealth creation for the benefit of employees, communities, the environment and investors. By ratcheting down the speed of speculation, a new corporate architecture can help investors escape the bone-rattling roller coaster of stock market volatility, bringing lower risk and more reliable long-term returns. Reducing capital pressure can enhance environmental and social performance, directing corporate decision-making in ways that avoid growth at any cost and abuse of ecological and human assets.

Alternative company designs are already functioning at many successful companies. Novo Nordisk, the Danish pharmaceutical company with revenues of €6 billion, is publicly traded yet owned by a foundation, allowing it to focus on its primary mission of defeating diabetes. Organic Valley, one of the largest organic brands in the USA with US$335 million in revenue, is a cooperative owned by the 1,200 farmers who produce its products. GrupoNueva in Santiago, Chile—a US$1.7 billion holding company founded by Stephan Schmidheiny, founder of the Business Council for Sustainable Development—is owned by the VIVA Trust, charged in perpetuity with maintaining the firm's vision and values. The John Lewis Partnership—the largest department store group in the UK, with US$9 billion in revenue—is 100% owned by its employees, and its stated purpose is serving the happiness of its employees. Alternative architectures work.

Principles of redesign

As our culture begins a dialogue aimed at shifting the predominant corporate architecture, we will encounter many choices. Design principles can provide a beacon. We can find comparable principles in the US Bill of Rights, the proposed European Union constitution, and the UN Universal Declaration of Human Rights, which are foundational principles that describe government's responsibilities to its citizenry.

In that spirit, Principles of Corporate Design have been drafted by Corporation 20/20, an initiative founded in 2004 as a multi-stakeholder process involving some 350 participants from business, finance, government, labour, law and civil society.[1] Its mission is to envision and advocate new corporate designs that embed social mission into the heart of organisations. Six principles form the pillars of the Corporation 20/20 vision:

▶ **Principle 1: Purpose.** The purpose of the corporation is to harness private interests to serve the public interest

▶ **Principle 2: Capital.** Corporations shall accrue fair returns for shareholders, but not at the expense of the legitimate interests of other stakeholders

▶ **Principle 3: Sustainability.** Corporations shall operate sustainably, meeting the needs of the present generation without compromising the ability of future generations to meet their needs

▶ **Principle 4: Wealth.** Corporations shall distribute their wealth equitably among those who contribute to wealth creation

▶ **Principle 5: Governance.** Corporations shall be governed in a manner that is participatory, transparent, ethical and accountable

▶ **Principle 6: Polity.** Corporations shall not infringe on the right of natural persons to govern themselves, nor infringe on other universal human rights

Prognosis

Creating new corporate architectures rooted in principles such as these does not depend solely on internal corporate initiatives, government mandates or civil society pressures. Only a combination of the three will work. Instead of the polarising lens of mandatory versus voluntary initiatives, there is a pathway that can be called 'facilitated internalisation'. In this model, standards are set by government, flexible compliance is undertaken by corporations and vigilance is provided by civil society empowered by formal access to decision-making.

Approaches such as these, based on a compelling new vision of corporate purpose, can point the way to transformed corporate design. The ultimate aim is to release the unparalleled capacity of the corporation to create long-term wealth, and to contribute to the great challenges of sustainable development that lie ahead. This is the design imperative of the 21st century.

References

Kelly, M., and A. White (2008) 'Corporate Design: The Missing Business and Public Policy Issue of Our Day', *New England Law Review* 42.4: 761-86.

Margolis, J.D., H.A. Elfenbein and J.P. Walsh (2008) 'Do Well by Doing Good? Don't Count on It', *Harvard Business Review* 86.1 (January 2008): 19.

Reich, R.B. (2007) *Supercapitalism: The Transformation of Business, Democracy, and Everyday Life* (New York: Alfred Knopf).

---

1 www.corporation2020.org, accessed 15 January 2009.

Vogel, D. (2008) 'The Market for Virtue Revisited', presentation at the John F. Kennedy School of Government, Harvard University, Cambridge, MA, 6 March 2008.

White, A.L. (2006) 'Transforming the Corporation', Great Transition Initiative, GTI Paper Series No. 5, www.gtinitiative.org/resources/paperseries.html, accessed 15 January 2009.

Allen L. White is co-founder and Director of Corporation 20/20. He co-founded the Global Reporting Initiative and was its CEO from 1999 to 2002. White is a senior fellow at Tellus Institute and senior adviser to Business for Social Responsibility.

✉ Tellus Institute, 11 Arlington St, Boston, MA 02116, USA

💻 awhite@tellus.org

Marjorie Kelly is co-founder of Corporation 20/20. She was co-founder and for 20 years the publisher of *Business Ethics* magazine. She is author of *The Divine Right of Capital* and senior associate at Tellus Institute.

✉ Tellus Institute, 11 Arlington St, Boston, MA 02116, USA

💻 mkelly@tellus.org

BUSINESS AS
AN AGENT OF
WORLD BENEFIT
MANAGE BY DESIGNING IN
AN ERA OF MASSIVE INNOVATION

The 2009 Global Forum for Business as an Agent of World Benefit
'Manage by Designing in an Era of Massive Innovation'

Join over 600 CEOs, managers, designers, and academics to explore how
Sustainability + Design = Value Creation
in an interactive and action-oriented forum

June 2–5, 2009
Case Western Reserve University
Cleveland, Ohio

Register at www.globalforum2009.com

Facilitated by
David Cooperrider, Weatherhead School of Management

Co-convened by
The Center for Business as an Agent of World Benefit (BAWB), Weatherhead School of Management
United Nations Global Compact (UNGC)
Academy of Management's Division of ODC

Sponsored by
The Fetzer Institute
Fairmount Minerals
CNI: The Brazilian National Confederation of Industry

Highlights of the Event

- Discover value drivers that work in today's global economic crisis
- Converse with peers from all sectors in a forum that is $^2/_3$ interactive and uses Appreciative Inquiry to focus dialogue and generate action
- Connect with UNGC, a network of 4,700 companies, including Accenture, CA, Coca-Cola, Cisco Systems, Deloitte, DuPont, eBay, Ford, Gap, HP, KPMG, Levis, Lexmark, Microsoft, Nike, Pepsi, Pfizer, PwC, Starbucks, and Sun Microsystems
- Participate in corporate-focused workshops, that include Ford, Cisco, Systems, Herman Miller, and Patagonia
- Attend a CEO panel that will ensure a practical and business-focused dialogue with Ray Anderson, CEO of Interface Inc., and Toby Cosgrove, CEO of Cleveland Clinic
- Discuss cutting-edge ideas from top management schools: Kellogg, Wharton, Rotterdam, Drucker, Rotman, Ross, Haas, Oxford's Said, Copenhagen, Carroll, and Weatherhead
- Hear inspiring talks by UNGC Executive Director Georg Kell, cradle-to-cradle architect Bill McDonough, UN Development Goals economist Jeffrey Sachs, biomimicry expert Janine Benyus, and other global leaders
- Be a part of post-Forum outputs. The 2006 Global Forum resulted in the United Nations Principles for Responsible Management Education (PRME), an initiative changing the field of management by inspiring and championing responsible management education, research, and thought leadership globally

Turning Point

The Amnesty International UK Business Group

Putting Human Rights on the Corporate Agenda

Sir Geoffrey Chandler

THE PRIVATISATION OF THE WORLD economy which followed the ending of the Cold War made the corporate sector a more important international influence on human rights for good or ill than almost any other constituency. Through its spreading supply chains it touched directly the lives of millions. Its operations affected the social and physical environment wherever it worked. Directly or indirectly it influenced the political scene. Unlike the environmental movement, however, which had long recognised the potential importance of companies and had for many years engaged in dialogue with them, the human rights movement was very slow to react. Human rights organisations had sporadically exposed and condemned direct corporate involvement in violations, but made no attempt to recruit the influence of the corporate world for the protection of human rights, although there was an obvious logic in harnessing the influence of entities which increasingly formed the bloodstream of the international economy. Indeed, companies and the human rights non-governmental organisations (NGOs) viewed each other with mutual ignorance, prejudice, suspicion and hostility. If we were to respond to the challenge presented by this new world, we needed somehow to cross this divide, finding a common language with which to engage in dialogue and create a mutual understanding.

In 1991 a small group of Amnesty members with business or industrial experience formed the Amnesty UK Business Group. The group started with a clear, if generalised purpose, which was set out in a Statement of Intent in November 1991. Its stated aims were 'to make the business community in the UK more aware of human rights issues around the world in the belief that corporate management can help to put an end to human rights abuses' and to 'encourage companies and business people involved in overseas trade and investment to use their international links to work for an improvement in human rights'. The statement added that the group:

> does not call for disinvestment or sanctions against governments or other bodies guilty of human rights violations. Similarly it takes no stand on the legitimacy of economic relations between such a government and organisations which have a commercial relationship with it.

It offered help to companies in the form of information on international human rights law and the human rights situation in countries in which they operated, assistance with company education programmes to raise awareness of the issues, and the organisation of urgent action appeals for employees or associates who might become victims overseas.

The foundations underlying the group's approach were that companies contributed much to the benefit of the world, that the best of them had their own principles, and that those who worked in them were no more or less moral than ourselves. But, if a company did harm in carrying out its business, if it failed to do the good within its legitimate power, then it would rightly be condemned. We wanted companies not only to avoid harm, but also to give positive support to human rights. We needed to expand companies' perceptions of their legitimate responsibilities; to reconcile conflicting views: ours that human rights were the business of business; theirs that they were not.

We had to make a fundamental decision. We were well aware of company abuses and those who suffered from them. But should we use what few resources we had in seeking out abuses? Or should we seek to remove the causes of abuse by influencing company policies and practice so that support for human rights would be applicable across the entirety of their operations? We chose the latter.

Amnesty was regarded with suspicion by companies. To counter this, we recruited as sponsors Richard Branson, Baroness Jean Denton, Sir John Harvey-Jones, Sir Peter Parker, Sir Lewis Robertson, Anita Roddick and Michael Stoddart, all of whom willingly signed the Statement of Intent and allowed us the use of their names. The group was launched at a dinner in November 1991 by Douglas Hurd, Foreign Secretary of the Conservative Government of the day.

We faced a problem in that Amnesty's traditional way of working was through protest and time-limited campaigns, whereas ours would be a long haul through engagement. Moreover Amnesty's attitude to the corporate sector was conditioned by an adversarial ethos derived from dealing with human rights abuses. Our initiative was therefore regarded with official indifference which was reflected in a minimum of administrative support which was later to dwindle to nothing. But this indifference also left us free to work from first principles, to experiment by trial and error unfettered by constraints. Indeed, for a time the group, its work done chiefly by volunteers,[1] operated as a semi-independent NGO, recognised as such by the outside world, and this was to be its strength.

The group's targets were the 50 or 60 major UK-based transnational companies (TNCs) which included some of the biggest in the world. We were initially naive. We thought that we could blow the trumpet and the walls of Jericho would fall. But Joshua was not a good role model. Letters to the chairmen of all these companies asking if we could come and discuss the issues and if they would be prepared to become 'companies in correspondence' with us met a polite but universal negative. The reply of the Chairman of BP in April 1992, 'I am afraid you are asking me to stand at the top of a very slippery slope', exemplified the responses. Human rights— then seen by all to be the civil and political rights which had led to Amnesty's founding—were for governments, not for companies.

We learned that a generic approach, engaging companies through correspondence alone, was a failure, that specific approaches on particular countries could provoke a wider response, and that we had to sharpen our objectives. In 1992 the group wrote to UK companies working in South Africa with a briefing on the situa-

---

1 The group comprised people acting in their individual capacity from academe, consultancies, socially responsible investment and accountancy, together with human rights lawyers and Amnesty members retired from business or industry.

tion there. This produced an appreciative response from a number of them with a promise to circulate it, but no undertaking in regard to action. The letter included the hope that 'one day it will be as much a source of pride for companies to say that they are an influence for the better in the human rights field as they are eager to claim today in the environmental field'. But that day had clearly not come.

In early 1993 we circulated to companies an Amnesty report on torture in China, offering to come and discuss its implications for their own operations. All replied, but none felt it appropriate to discuss the issues. A few expressed appreciation of the briefing and their sympathy. One or two chairmen admitted to personal membership of Amnesty. The majority view was reflected in the response of the chairman of British American Tobacco: 'We operate worldwide and we do not comment on such matters as human rights violations. It is inappropriate for us to do so, particularly as the environment in which we operate is so variable.' The most positive response was that of Trafalgar House: 'As a company which operates in almost every country of the world we are very aware of the need to demonstrate our commitment to human rights.' The least positive that of Rolls Royce: 'The report does not correlate with our own information and experiences in China over more than thirty years. I do not believe any useful purpose would be served by a meeting.'

We were not getting through, even though there was growing awareness of our existence. In early 1994 a UK business delegation to China, well aware of the country's huge economic promise, but not of its human rights violations, prompted us to clarify our targets which became:

▶ Explicit corporate commitment to human rights based on the Universal Declaration of Human Rights (UDHR)

▶ Operationalising that commitment

▶ Subjecting it to independent audit

We argued that a distinction needed to be made between, on the one hand, interfer-ence in political matters, which companies rightly saw as taboo, and on the other the ability to express condemnation of human rights violations. Our work on China stirred some interest, but there was still total corporate reluctance to engage.

In 1995 Shell changed the world for itself and for the work of the group. Reputational disaster, not corporate forethought, nor indeed our arguments, proved the catalyst for change. Shell's experience in Nigeria and, later, BP's in Colombia provided us with a platform and a breakthrough. The arbitrary execution of Ken Saro-Wiwa and eight other Ogonis by the Nigerian dictatorship of General Abacha in November 1995 is a story that does not need retelling. The insistence of Shell, the largest foreign oil company in Nigeria and the operator, though minority shareholder, of its partnership with the Nigerian government, that it was improper for the company to play any role in trying to deflect the course of events, led to international condemnation. While the potential influence of the company was certainly exaggerated, its silence until the last moment could find no justification and the accusation of complicity with an oppressive regime which the company's activities helped to sustain proved overwhelming to the reputation of one of the most sophisticated and respected companies in the world. Shell's arguments for inaction stemmed from the belief that to intervene would imply a breach of its existing principles which called for the avoidance of involvement in domestic politics. The failure to perceive the difference between such politics, which rightly should be immune from corporate influence, and human rights, which transcend national boundaries, lay at the root of the situation, just as it had underlain the responses that we had earlier received from companies. Indeed, the UDHR, with its injunction for 'all individuals and organs of society' to give their support, was unknown to companies, as it was to most of the world, but was now to become our key weapon in seeking a change of attitudes.

Our approach to Shell had begun with

protest—a delegation to Shell Centre at which we met the Chairman of the Committee of Managing Directors—and almost every NGO brought pressure to bear. In an unprecedented confession of corporate culpability Shell admitted it had not kept pace with the views of society. The company asked for our help and 1996 saw a long period of engagement in the UK and in the Netherlands, where representatives of Amnesty International Nederland and Pax Christi also played a role.[2] This was a learning process for both sides, engendering mutual trust and respect without which it would have been difficult to move forward constructively. Shell now systematically examined the core values that should underpin its business and how these should be interpreted into a revision of the company's Statement of General Business Principles which had been first formulated in 1976. Discussions continued over a period of many months. The fact that we were meeting the company was public knowledge, but we respected the company's wish to treat the detail of the discussions in confidence which enabled them to be fully open with us on the development of their thinking and to seek advice on both drafting and implementation.

As a result of this, in March 1997 support for human rights was explicitly embedded in Shell's Statement of General Business Principles. This now included a responsibility to respect the human rights of employees and 'to express support for fundamental human rights in line with the legitimate role of business'. While the UDHR underlay the Statement and was mentioned in supporting documents, it did not feature in the Statement itself. While some argued for this, it was for us the beginning of recognition that the very broad obligations of the UDHR could not be imposed on business without being interpreted in a manner that related to the business sphere of influence—an issue which has been central to the debate ever since. Similar discussions were now taking place with BP, whose security arrangements in Colombia had come under intense public criticism for their alleged contribution to human rights violations, and in March 1998 BP also published a revised set of business policies. These, entitled *What we stand for . . .* , incorporated explicit support for the principles of the UDHR.

We could now approach other companies not only with the UDHR, but also the example of two of the world's most respected companies. And peer example we knew would make more impact than NGO preaching. We therefore planned a systematic approach to other major TNCs, our next converts being Rio Tinto, which had also suffered reputational damage, and BT, which had not.

There were a number of arguments which shifted formerly entrenched positions: the demonstrable cost to reputation of getting it wrong, the applicability to companies of the UDHR, a document of which they had been previously unaware, the argument that silence on human rights was not neutrality, and that we were asking companies not to criticise governments, but to support internationally agreed values. It was labour-intensive work. We had to understand the imperatives of business and gain the respect of those with whom we talked. We had to win the argument of principle and then assist the development of policies. The 'business case'—the cost to reputation—might be the way in, but it was important to remember that the business case is fundamentally amoral and cannot begin to cover the totality of a company's operations.

The process of engagement taught us to recognise our own inadequacies, in particular the failure so far to produce clear human rights guidelines for companies

---

2 See Lawrence 2002 for an admirably intelligent analysis of the dialogue between Shell and the human rights organisations, though the theoretical framework built to understand the conditions that drive corporate–stakeholder engagement probably overstates the organisational coherence on the NGO side.

and the weakness of tackling the essentially international challenge that TNCs offered on a purely national basis. Companies feared that the adoption of human rights policies might put them at a competitive disadvantage with those that did not and asked if Amnesty was taking international action, to which the answer was: no. The first we could remedy and were shortly to do so; but Amnesty's failure to confront the corporate challenge internationally remains a continuing problem today.

We realised that, with engagement, needed to go other mutually reinforcing activities. We needed to create a climate of opinion by getting the issues into the public domain and therefore spoke publicly to a variety of audiences on every occasion offered. We needed to use the 'multipliers': for example, we approached the business schools, almost exclusively followers of Milton Friedman in their teaching, and argued for a broadening of their curriculum. We encouraged the involvement of consultancies and professional bodies. We forged ad hoc alliances with like-minded NGOs. We did not abandon protest as a weapon. But while protest can raise issues, it takes engagement to win the argument.

In early 1996 we had produced a further briefing paper on China, but again the action we asked for was in very general terms: explicit support for the UDHR, a declaration of intent to maintain internationally accepted employment standards and to deal only with suppliers who adhere to such standards, a willingness to exercise quiet influence within the country without jeopardising the company's commercial interests. But companies are pragmatic entities, wanting to know in detail what they are committing themselves to. This we finally provided in 1997 in *Human Rights Guidelines for Companies* (Amnesty International UK Business Group 1997), the first publication of its kind, which remains a useful document to this day. This spelt out the direct responsibility of companies for the protection of human rights in their own operations and

provided a checklist of the human rights principles which were applicable to them. It included sections on policy and strategic planning, personnel policies and practices, and security arrangements, extending the meaning of human rights for companies from the narrow interpretation of only civil and political rights to the broader spectrum which has now become accepted. It moreover made clear, which many international lawyers still fail to do, that companies' responsibility for their impact on human rights exists regardless of the obligations of states. The publication provided a useful entrée to companies as a prelude to engagement. Requests from Amnesty sections in other countries led to an immediate international circulation.

In 1997 we held, in Birmingham, the first public conference on business and human rights. Chaired by Sir Adrian Cadbury, one of the UK's most distinguished industrialists, this was attended by companies, NGOs and government representatives and we used the occasion for the launch of *Human Rights Guidelines for Companies*. This broke a barrier and opened the way for a succession of conferences in universities and institutions on the subject of human rights and corporate responsibility.

Amnesty's support for the group ended at this point. But, unsolicited, Joel Joffe, the organiser of the defence of Nelson Mandela and his co-defendants at the Rivonia trial, offered us most generous financial help from his charitable trust and sustained our work for three and a half years. This enabled us to recruit Peter Frankental as a staff member who provided a superbly constructive administrative base for what had been till then a predominantly voluntary effort. We were now able to conduct a systematic approach to companies, including financial institutions for the first time, and to produce publications that could help spread awareness of the issues and provide constructive assistance. These included briefing for pension funds, a brief on Saudi Arabia and a geography of corporate risk which has since been widely copied and expanded by others. Most importantly, in April 2000, a management guide, *Human Rights: Is it any of your business?* (Frankental and House 2000) was produced jointly with the Prince of Wales International Business Leaders' Forum and had the advantage of now being able to include case studies from companies that had embraced human rights. In 2002 the single-page geography of corporate risk was expanded to illustrate the international risk exposure to human rights violations of companies in six major industrial sectors and was launched simultaneously in London, Brussels, Stockholm and New York. We responded to requests from Amnesty national branches in other countries to talk to their transnational companies for which they felt themselves to have no capability.

The Business Group had created a bridgehead for human rights in the corporate world. The genie was out of the bottle: human rights were now on all agendas and initiatives proliferated. All raised the profile of the debate, and, even though any self-sustaining momentum would be slow to come, there would be no retreat. The Business Group now became one of many entities engaged in promoting human rights. It continued to play a part in the debate, to engage with companies, and to look in detail at particular areas, such as host-government agreements, in which human rights could be at risk.

Had the group not existed, other influences—the increasing corporate experience of conflict and violations, the power of the Internet and the outlet for protest it provided—would eventually have brought change. What the group did was to hasten that change. When it closed down in 2007 its pioneering work had been completed.

References

Amnesty International UK Business Group (1997) *Human Rights Guidelines for Companies* (London: Amnesty International UK Business Group, repr. 1998 and 2000).

Frankental, P., and F. House (2000) *Human Rights: Is it any of your business?* (London: Amnesty International UK/Prince of Wales Business Leaders' Forum).

Lawrence, A.T. (2002) 'The Drivers of Stakeholder Engagement: Reflections on the Case of Royal Dutch/Shell', *Journal of Corporate Citizenship* 6 (April 2002): 71-85.

Sir **Geoffrey Chandler** CBE is Chair Emeritus of the Amnesty International UK Business Group, having been Founder-Chair from 1991 to 2001. He spent 22 years with the Royal Dutch/Shell Group where he was a Director of Shell International and the initiator of Shell's first Statement of General Business Principles in 1976. He was Director General of the UK National Economic Development Office 1978–83 and chaired the National Council of Voluntary Organisations 1989–96.

✉ Little Gaterounds, Newdigate, Dorking RH5 5AJ, UK

🖥 geoffchand@AOL.com

Making a Difference?

Corporate Responsibility as a Social Movement*

Sandra Waddock

Boston College, Carroll School of Management, USA

This paper explores the ways in which the current emphasis on corporate responsibility constitutes a social movement by using the elements that constitute social movements to illustrate how a group of pioneers created new organisations and institutions that push companies in the direction of greater accountability, responsibility and transparency. According to sociologists Doug McAdam, John McCarthy and Mayer Zald, social movements have three core elements: framing processes, political opportunity structures and mobilising structures. The paper illustrates the ways in which individuals, here called the difference makers (along with many others, of course), used these three aspects of social movements to forward greater attention to issues of corporate responsibility over several decades and in a wide variety of ways.

● Difference makers

● Corporate responsibility movement

● Corporate citizenship

● Social entrepreneurs

● Institutional entrepreneurs

● Social movement

Sandra Waddock is the Galligan Chair of Strategy and Professor of Management at Boston College's Carroll School of Management, and Senior Research Fellow at BC's Center for Corporate Citizenship. Widely published on corporate responsibility and citizenship, she holds MBA and DBA degrees from Boston University.

✉ Boston College, Carroll School of Management, Chestnut Hill, MA 02467, USA

🖳 waddock@bc.edu

* This article is partially excerpted from Sandra Waddock, *The Difference Makers: How Social and Institutional Entrepreneurs Created the Corporate Responsibility Movement* (Sheffield, UK: Greenleaf Publishing, 2008).

N THE LAST SEVERAL DECADES OF THE 20TH CENTURY, CONTINUING TO TODAY, social and institutional entrepreneurs, here called the difference makers (see Waddock 2008b), have built the foundations of a corporate responsibility movement that is attempting to push corporations in the direction of greater accountability, responsibility and transparency. This paper will focus on social movements as a way of understanding how the current emphasis on corporate responsibility has emerged over the past several decades. A more complete version of this story is told in *The Difference Makers: How Social and Institutional Entrepreneurs Created the Corporate Responsibility Movement* (Greenleaf Publishing, 2008). This paper specifically explores how the establishment of new institutions helped difference makers constitute the new movement we can call the corporate responsibility movement.

Twenty-three 'difference makers', leading thinkers, activists and social and institutional entrepreneurs who have built well-known pioneering organisations, or done other foundational work around issues of corporate responsibility, were interviewed for this research. All of them are leaders in developing what has elsewhere been termed a corporate responsibility infrastructure (Waddock 2008a). These difference makers established a range of pioneering organisations and institutions that explicitly attempted to effect system change that would bring corporations in line with the social and ecological imperatives that difference makers and their constituencies perceived but which represent considerably different imperatives from the typical financial and economic imperatives that drive much thinking about the modern corporation. All of the difference makers can be considered activists. Unlike social activists working to change the system from outside as many NGOs, interest groups and pressure groups do, the difference makers have attempted to effect change from a position that is at the interstice between business and society, neither fully within business nor fully outside.

A social movement?

The question at the core of this paper is: does the focus on corporate responsibility (shorthand for accountability, responsibility and transparency) today in fact constitute a social movement? In what follows, I will argue that the leadership of difference makers in establishing a wide range of new organisations and institutions provided a foundation for numerous similar entities that now constitute a vast and still growing landscape of groups attempting to foster greater corporate responsibility. This emphasis on corporate responsibility does in fact represent a social movement. Social movements, according to sociologists Doug McAdam, John McCarthy and Mayer Zald (1996), have three core elements: framing processes, political opportunity structures and mobilising structures. In various ways, as will be explored below, difference makers used all three elements to construct the corporate responsibility movement.

Framing processes

Framing processes indicate that there is a debate or conversation going on between parties with different views, each trying to shape the conversation in what is a contested field (McAdam *et al.* 1996). In the case of corporate responsibility, that contest exists between the proponents of the neoclassical economic model (e.g. Milton Friedman whose famous *New York Times* headline in 1970 proclaimed 'the business of business is to make a profit'; Friedman 1970), free trade and globalisations, and the difference makers (among many others) who believe that corporations should serve a broader, more public purpose, and should in doing so be more accountable, responsible and transparent. For years, Friedman advocated a strict free-market ideology, which has, according to some observers, become embedded in many places in the world, sometimes to the detriment of societal interests (e.g. Klein 2007). The difference makers perceived a need for a different way for corporations to interact with society—with greater responsibility, accountability and transparency. Arguably, each in his or her own way built entities or thought leaders to leverage change in that direction.

Of course, as with all social movements, the timing or zeitgeist needs to be right for the evolution of the movement; typically multiple actors move towards a similar goal simultaneously, even if initially their efforts are disconnected (see, for example, Paul Hawken's (2008) wonderful description of the evolution of what he terms 'blessed unrest', or a move towards Earth- and people-centred values, in his book by that title). Thus, what we see in the framing processes are a number of actors—social and institutional entrepreneurs—beginning to move at approximately the same time.

We begin this story, however, with one individual and one organisation, specifically focused on the issue of corporate responsibility. In the early stages of the corporate responsibility movement, the focus of activity began with the Council on Economic Priorities (CEP), founded in 1969 by difference maker Alice Tepper Marlin (who later founded Social Accountability International), which 'named names' and published research on social issues linked to companies during the 1970s. Then, in the mid-1980s, CEP developed a book called *Rating America's Corporate Conscience* with difference maker Steve Lydenberg (currently with Domini Social Investments; co-founder, KLD Research & Analytics, and the Institute for Responsible Investing at the Boston College Center for Corporate Citizenship) as lead author (Lydenberg *et al.* 1986).

In the late 1980s, *Rating America's Corporate Conscience*, which had been the first systematic attempt at evaluating the social performance of a wide range of brand-name, consumer-oriented companies, morphed into a pocket-sized consumers' guide called *Shopping for a Better World*. This guide helped consumers make pro-social choices with respect to consumer goods by providing new information that helped frame purchasing behaviour differently. Notably, in the United Kingdom, difference maker John Elkington, who later founded one of the first consulting firms in the corporate responsibility space, SustainAbility, also published the *Green Consumer Guide* (Elkington and Hailes 1988) during this same period.

Other pioneering efforts during this early period included the founding of the Interfaith Center on Corporate Responsibility (ICCR) in 1971, of which difference maker Tim Smith (now with Walden Asset Management, and formerly president of the Social Investment Forum) was the founding executive director. ICCR made the first organised efforts to submit shareholder resolutions seeking corporate changes on a regular basis. These social and environmental shareholder resolutions, which had been pioneered in 1970 as part of an activist campaign against General Motors, grew of out 1960s anti-corporate activism. Typically, social shareholder resolutions, which are submitted by shareholders and thus represent an 'insider' strategy, call on targeted companies' management to change specific company practices that the religious investors behind the ICCR considered problematic.

To this day ICCR, now a coalition of some 275 religiously affiliated investor groups, issues more than 200 shareholder resolutions annually on a broad array of topics ranging from environment to sweatshop labour to anti-discrimination, and this type of activism has been picked up by numerous other activists with similar agendas. Such initiatives, like the social investment movement itself, began to reframe the debate about what the responsibilities of corporations were by focusing attention on specific issues that went beyond maximisation of shareholder wealth—with questions about these issues actually coming from investors, much to management's chagrin. In particular during the 1980s shareholder activism gained a lot of momentum and visibility by focusing on changing or dismantling the apartheid regime in South Africa. Later shareholder resolutions broadened to issues that social investors considered to be socially problematic, including products such as cigarettes, gaming and military contracting; ultimately various stakeholder practices such as supply chain management and employee policies also began to be targeted. Over time, as society has changed, so have the issues on which shareholder resolutions focus.

Such reframing of corporate responsibilities continues to evolve, today emphasising how companies can better serve societies, nature and the variety of stakeholders who make investments in them. More analytically sound and rigorous approaches to social investment began to emerge during the 1980s, as means of evaluating corporations, and specific issues crystallised. Early proponents of social investment included Joan Bavaria (founder, Trillium Asset Management, Ceres, Social Investment Forum and the Investor Network on Climate Change, as well as key sponsor of the Global Reporting Initiative), Amy Domini (founder, Domini Social Funds and co-founder KLD Research and Analytics) and Alice Tepper Marlin when she was one of the pioneering women on Wall Street. When these women listened to their clients, they realised that for some investors factors other than wealth maximisation, social factors in particular, were also important. This recognition triggered ideas that framed new thinking about how investors might profitably invest yet still keep social purposes in mind.

The early days of socially responsible investing (SRI), which in many ways seeded the larger movement, were largely about framing and developing the fundamentals of social investment strategies, which take what are today known as environmental, social and governance (ESG) issues into account along with financial performance. As several of the difference makers involved in SRI noted, some investors wanted to lead with their values but there were no systematic ways of doing that. Early on, social investment decisions were made on a company-by-company basis, typically on an exclusionary basis. For instance, some religious investors wanted to avoid companies that did military contracting, while others wished to avoid cigarette manufacturers or nuclear involvement. As noted above, for many during the 1980s, dismantling the apartheid regime in South Africa, through disinvestment in companies participating there, became a critical focus. While it was possible to screen out companies with such products, the lack of systematic approaches that provided information on the range of companies available to social investors was a major impediment to the growth of this segment of the investment industry.

In one sense, SRI serves as a counterpart to traditional investing by attempting to leverage traditional mechanisms associated with investors for social benefit, while simultaneously reframing for investors the importance of taking ESG issues into account. Today, of course, as we will explore below, there is a vast infrastructure supporting the SRI elements of the corporate responsibility movement, and proponents of SRI claim that some one in nine investment dollars is in some sort of socially active investment (Social Investment Forum 2008). For traditional investors, responsibility is simply assumed to mean wealth maximisation within the constraints of the law, while for social investors, as several difference makers pointed out in interviews, it means investing in alignment with one's values. Early advocates of SRI were reframing the debate to encompass other issues, issues that we might today call stakeholder and sustainability issues. As this reframing was happening, other areas of corporate responsibility and other approaches to pressuring companies for better behaviour began to evolve, particularly as various difference makers saw new opportunities in the gaps between what they perceived to be reality and what was socially desirable. To do SRI well, however, required the development of new mechanisms and systemic approaches and also ultimately meant that issues of accountability and transparency were necessarily taken into account as well as responsibility. Doing that meant moving towards the second element of social movements by tapping into existing and developing new 'opportunity structures' and beginning to address specific gaps.

Opportunity structures

Opportunity structures are the established order in the existing political, social and institutional environment, with which any movement must contend, but where gaps and opportunities that can be tapped by the right social entrepreneur exist (McAdam *et al.* 1996). Typically applied to the political domain, this concept of political opportunity structures suggests that social movements face existing political arrangements that can either enhance or inhibit mobilisation of resources around the relevant movement. In the case of the corporate responsibility movement, the surrounding opportunity structures were more associated with business as usual, within companies, in the investment community, and with respect to social expectations from companies.

As the SRI field began to develop, one important gap was clear to Amy Domini, Peter Kinder and Steve Lydenberg, who co-founded the social research firm KLD Research & Analytics in 1990. The need for better, more systemically gathered and consistent data had become clear to Domini after she wrote one of the first books on social investing, called *Ethical Investing*, with Peter Kinder in 1986 (Domini and Kinder 1986), and suddenly found herself on the speaking circuit. People asked her two fundamental questions about SRI: What is social investing, and whose ethics are at work here as investment decisions are made? The second key question was: How much of a financial trade-off would the social investor have to make?[1]

KLD (then called Kinder, Lydenberg, Domini) tapped into Steve Lydenberg's experience in developing the research for and writing *Rating America's Corporate Conscience* at CEP. When launched, KLD became the pioneering social research firm for SRI. When the company launched its first data in 1991, it covered the entire Standard & Poor's 500 companies annually, gathering data along multiple dimensions of corporate responsibility performance, including traditional negative screens favoured by some investors, but also looking for both negative and progressive practices in other categories such as employees, products, international operations, community and environment. In the sense that it focused on various stakeholder and natural environmental practices with both positive and negative ratings, KLD went significantly beyond earlier efforts at evaluating companies, which simply screened out companies operating in particular domains.

The original idea behind KLD was to create an index that could be used to track performance against standard measures such as the Dow Jones Industrial Average, but what really kept the business alive was the research, which was sold to interested investors, at least until the index had proved its mettle. For the SRI and corporate responsibility movement more generally to go forward initially, then, involved a reframing of, for example, investors' expectations about the relationship between company performance and responsibility, and, ultimately, new ways of fostering accountability by corporations. Pressure was put on them for better performance by creating greater transparency about their activities, this pressure coming from social activists submitting shareholder resolutions or from more widely available data such as that supplied by KLD.

The proliferation of social rating agencies such as KLD in different countries, whose work is consolidated by the umbrella organisation, Sustainable Investment Research

---

1 Note that a good deal of research on this question suggests that there is, in fact, no financial trade-off.

International (SiRi Group), and the advent of other socially or environmentally oriented stock market indices (of which the Dow Jones Sustainability Index and the UK's FTSE4Good are but two examples) provide evidence of the institutionalisation of core SRI elements of the corporate responsibility movement. Further, the numerous professional and trade associations, magazines and conferences supporting SRI attests to the growth of this segment of the investment industry and the success of these pioneering entities in fostering similar entities on a global basis (see Waddock 2008a, for a detailed listing of some of these institutions).

The movement demanding greater corporate responsibility, however, did not stop with SRI. It had become clear by the middle of the 1990s that pressure from investors, while an important leverage point, was only one of the elements necessary to move corporations towards greater responsibility and, particularly, accountability for their actions. By the 1990s, globalisation was in full force and external activists, NGOs and pressure groups were making clear that the extended supply chains employed by many large multinational corporations were extremely problematic in terms of working conditions, labour standards, human rights and environmental protection.

As this activism grew, difference maker Alice Tepper Marlin became aware of another gap when her organisation, then the Council on Economic Priorities, wanted to create a students' guide to shopping for a better world. She realised that there was very little systematic data—or even understanding outside of companies—of what was happening in global supply chains, yet, as activists and NGOs were insisting vociferously, there were significant problems in those extended supply chains. At the global level, new networks of organisations with missions similar to CEP's had begun to form, partly under Tepper Marlin's initiative, based on common interests—part of the creation of mobilising structures, or networks of organisations in other nations doing similar work to that of CEP. But the difficulty of finding adequate data on what was happening in supply chains led to the founding of Social Accountability International (SAI) and the eventual dissolution of CEP.

In the morphing of CEP into what is now SAI, we can see a social entrepreneurial process, with Tepper Marlin building the network of individuals surrounding her, sensing a gap and ultimately seizing an opportunity to create an appropriate mobilising structure in the form of SAI. SAI focuses explicitly on labour standards and environmental standards in companies operating in developing countries, and has developed codes of conduct, monitoring and certification protocols for extended supply chains. The seeds of SAI's approach lie in other initiatives that are also part of the burgeoning corporate responsibility movement. For example, difference maker Bob Dunn had taken an important step at Levi-Strauss, where he was employed in the early 1990s, in leading the establishment of the first-ever company-based supplier code of conduct. As another example, the Caux Roundtable Principles (and similar initiatives on a global level, such as the Sullivan Principles) had been established in 1986 by a coalition of business leaders, and are now overseen by difference maker Steven B. Young. The Caux Principles also provided guidance about global standards of practice. As Tepper Marlin noted, one important innovation came from the ISO (International Organisation for Standardisation) quality and environmental standards, which served as a model for what SAI attempted to do in the domain of labour standards.

At about the same period of time in the UK, the attempt to establish greater corporate accountability also became the basis for the founding in 1995 of the Institute of Social and Ethical Accountability, better known simply as AccountAbility. Headed by Simon Zadek, AccountAbility, like KLD and SAI, attempts to create corporate accountability through metrics, measurement and other systematic data. Zadek had been involved in some of the earliest social audits of corporate performance (e.g. with The Body Shop and Ben & Jerry's), drawn from the work of the New Economics Foundation (NEF), where

Zadek was then working. NEF founded AccountAbility, driven in part by Zadek's inter-est in metrics, and also the Ethical Trading Initiative (ETI), a European counterpart to the US-based Fair Labor Association. The ETI and Fair Labor Association both attempted to hold companies accountable for their labour practices in developing nations, repre-senting new mechanisms of accountability created because of an opportunity structure that existed. Another consulting company, also one of the pioneers, was The Corporate Citizenship Company, now owned by the communications company Chime, founded by David Logan, who was also one of the co-authors of an early corporate citizenship report produced in 1997 by the Hitachi Foundation—a report that serves as something of a marker, providing a model for the many such reports to come.

Some of the seeds for holding corporations accountable for their actions in develop-ing nations had been planted much earlier. One prominent instance was the Nestlé boy-cott, which was generated because of the company's problematic practice of distributing infant formula to new mothers, who could not afford it nor had adequate sanitation to use it properly, in developing countries. Difference maker Jim Post of Boston Univer-sity had been one of the first academics (along with others such as Prakash Sethi of Baruch College in New York) to study the infant formula practices. For his seminal work on the infant formula problem, Post ended up as a member of the pioneering Nestlé Audit Commission, which was a first of its kind initiative formed to hold the company accountable for its distribution practices and overseen by an independent group of out-siders.

Other opportunities for creating greater corporate accountability lay in what became a rather extensive array of new standards, principles and codes of conduct that provide standards of business practice, of which we have already seen some examples. Of course, an early effort in this arena had been the OECD Guidelines for Multinational Corpora-tions, and another had been the Sullivan Principles, which articulated how companies should deal with involvement in South Africa during the apartheid era. As already men-tioned, Levi-Strauss had pioneered a supplier code of conduct in the early 1990s, which provided some insight into how issues might be dealt with from a company perspec-tive. Further, when the *Exxon Valdez* had spilled millions of gallons of oil in Alaska in 1989, difference maker Joan Bavaria and others seized the opportunity to name a set of environmental standards already in development the Valdez Principles (now renamed the Ceres Principles). Bavaria, who had earlier founded a pioneering social investment firm called Franklin Research and Development (now Trillium Asset Management), later founded Ceres, the Coalition for Environmentally Responsible Economies. Ceres provided what became the Ceres Principles and began signing up companies commit-ted to live up to those principles.

In 1999, then UN Secretary-General Kofi Annan attended the World Economic Forum in Davos, Switzerland, and called for a new 'compact' between business and society, in a speech drafted by difference makers John Ruggie (then Special Assistant to the Sec-retary-General, now a professor at Harvard's Kennedy School of Government and at the time of writing also Special Assistant to the UN Secretary-General for Human Rights and Business) and Georg Kell (then working at the UN at a junior level to Ruggie, now Executive Head of the UN Global Compact). Although initially Annan had not intended to create an actual initiative around the social compact that he had articulated, business response was so strong and positive that two years later, through the work of Ruggie and Kell, the UN Global Compact (UNGC) was launched. Clearly, Annan, through the work of Ruggie and Kell, had tapped into another gap: a need for an entity with global stature such as the United Nations to speak up from its 'bully pulpit' about the responsibilities of corporations to the societies that created and supported them.

The UNGC's ten principles have since framed what is characterised as the world's largest corporate citizenship initiative, with more than 4,000 corporate signatories at the time of writing (and well over 5,000 total signatories). Of course, along with the Global Compact, dozens of other standards and principles began emerging during this period. Further, hundreds, if not thousands, of companies have now developed their own internal codes of conduct, which, working with suppliers, they often seek to push down the supply chain. In addition, there are now numerous organisations that have issued more general sets of principles, codes of conduct and standards, some of which are industry-specific, by this point in time making it somewhat of an imperative particularly for large businesses to be associated with one or more such standards of practice.[2] Of course, these developments came about in part because of external activism by NGOs and interest groups, who were placing significant public attention on issues related to supply chain management and globalisation, but also in part because such initiatives had been modelled by some of the pioneers.

By the late 1990s, Bob Massie, who had become executive director of Ceres, with Allen White of Tellus Institute, who had worked on metrics pro bono for Ceres as it developed the Ceres Principles, sensed another opportunity. In effect, the pair identified another gap in standardised reporting for environmental, social and governance (ESG) issues. Recognising the importance of the common metric of the financial report, which follows generally accepted accounting principles (GAAP), they determined that what was needed was a similar common framework around ESG. The result of that insight was the founding, with Ceres's backing, of the Global Reporting Initiative (GRI), which created a 'big tent' in the words of Allen White, and brought in a wide range of stakeholders to help with its development, thereby enhancing buy-in even from critics. GRI has since become the de facto global standard for standardised ESG reporting.

Of course, gaps continue to exist and numerous new entities and institutions continue to be developed by the difference makers and, of course, many, many others. But as these early institutions evolved, so did mechanisms and means for mobilising the many others interested in the same types of issue through what are called mobilising structures, the third core element of social movements.

Mobilising structures

Mobilising structures involve the use or creation of networks of interested parties, including individuals and organisations, some of which are newly created to tap into the opportunities identified by social entrepreneurs, to move the social movement's agenda forward (McAdam *et al.* 1996). Mobilising structures in the political domain might be activist organisations, protest groups, or in recent years use of the Internet to foment action on a cause. Of course, all of these vehicles have been used by various groups in the anti-globalisation and anti-corporate movements. The difference makers created their own mobilisation structures via linkages with each other in trade and professional associations, networks of forward-looking businesses and other types of alliance. These alliances, networks and coalitions served the functions of creating positive role models, exerting peer pressure, raising issues and providing forums for learning, dialogue and the generation of new insights about accountability, responsibility, transparency and, increasingly, sustainability. One early example of such a mobilising structure in the corporate responsibility arena was the formation of a professional association for SRI, the Social Investment Forum (SIF) in 1981, by difference maker Joan

---

2 Some would claim, of course, that simply signing on to a code is insufficient and may in fact be nothing more than window dressing. Nonetheless, it is clear that some of the most progressive companies take these codes very seriously and are working hard to integrate the principles and values stated in them into their strategies and practices.

Bavaria with others. SIF is now the leading US-based professional association for social investors, and has counterparts in both the UK and Europe.

Such networks, professional associations and alliances include the Boston College Center for Corporate Citizenship (CCC), founded in 1986 by Edmund Burke as the Center for Corporate Community Relations, and converted into the broader agenda CCC by difference maker Brad Googins in the late 1990s. Another very important such mobilising structure in the US is Business for Social Responsibility (BSR), founded in 1991, derived from New England Business for Social Responsibility, which was established in 1988 by difference maker Laury Hammel (CEO of Longfellow Clubs in the Greater Boston area). BSR was later expanded and refocused on large companies by difference maker Bob Dunn, who ran it for many years. With the refocusing of BSR on large businesses and away from small businesses such as his own, Hammel went on to establish other networks that also serve as mobilising structures, including co-founding the BALLE, the Business Alliance for Local Living Economies, which now has chapters throughout the United States, and also the annual International Symposium on Spirituality in Business.

Similar networks have proliferated. For example, difference makers David Grayson and Jane Nelson have been involved in the UK's Business in the Community and the International Business Leaders Forum, and difference maker Malcolm McIntosh held several of the first conversations on corporate citizenship at the University of Warwick, while he served as first hired director of the Corporate Citizenship Unit at Warwick University (the Unit had been created by former executive Chris Marsden) in the early 2000s. More recently, McIntosh continues his thought leadership in his post at Coventry University, where he has been organising conferences aimed at rethinking the global economic system to enhance social justice, sustainability, peace and security. The dozens and dozens of conferences, multi-stakeholder dialogues, colloquia, academic centres and even whole programmes around issues of corporate responsibility that have proliferated around the globe attest to the rapid growth of these ideas—as well as to the solid foundation on which the corporate responsibility movement now stands.

That networks serve as mobilising structures is highlighted even more by the work that difference maker Steve Waddell has done in establishing the Global Action Network-Network (GAN-net). GAN-net is an entity that brings together the work of other networks with global scope and attempts to help them do their work more effectively. As an entity GAN-net links people in networks such as the Forest Stewardship Council or the Ethical Trading Initiative (see www.gan-net.net for a listing of the numerous GANs identified by GAN-net) with others in GANs so that they can learn how to better manage their GAN as an organisation and have more impact in their work.

Other mobilising structures involve establishing centres such as the Corporate Social Responsibility Initiative at Harvard's Kennedy School of Government, directed by difference maker Jane Nelson, which provides a kind of 'bully pulpit' at a notable university for issues related to corporate responsibility. Hundreds of universities have now established similar centres with titles ranging from business ethics to corporate social responsibility to corporate citizenship. Malcolm McIntosh of Coventry University founded the *Journal of Corporate Citizenship* (while he was at Warwick University) in 2001 to provide a scholarly/practitioner outlet for thinking about corporate responsibility and to help shape the debate. Numerous academic and practice-based publications now exist that highlight the work of corporate responsibility, some of which had been established earlier, but took on new life with the growth of the movement, and others that are new and try to reach different audiences.

A few universities have even established programmes on corporate responsibility or sustainability, pushed in part by the attention that the work of difference maker Judith Samuelson has brought to bear on management education. Samuelson established what is now the Aspen Institute's Business and Society Program, which has focused explicitly on bringing sustainability and responsibility issues into management education, through ratings such as the Beyond Grey Pinstripes ranking of business schools on sustainability and business in society dimensions, the Faculty Pioneer Awards, which highlight the work of academics in the corporate responsibility arena, and others surveys of MBA graduates that have received considerable public attention.

Another example of an explicit mobilising structure is the Institute for Responsible Investing (IRI), the brainchild of KLD co-founder Steve Lydenberg within the Boston College Center for Corporate Citizenship. A small institute, initially operating under the radar on a shoestring budget, the IRI specifically focused on convening thought leaders around issues that were important to SRI but that had no forum in which to be heard: for example, the responsibility implications of mergers and acquisitions, real estate development and the bond markets.

Finally, a forward-looking mobilising structure was developed by difference maker Allen White of Tellus Institute with collaborator Marjorie Kelly, also of Tellus and former editor of *Business Ethics* magazine, which had created the Best 100 Corporate Citizens ranking.[3] This initiative is called Corporation 20/20 and it is an explicit multi-stakeholder effort, drawing on some of the learning that came from establishing the GRI, about how to 'build a big tent' to incorporate many stakeholders with differing ideas, to use White's words. Corporation 20/20's goal is to rethink and re-purpose the corporation to better meet 21st-century needs. It brings together thought leaders around these important questions and launched a major conference in Boston's famed Faneuil Hall in 2007 to openly address these questions. Such initiatives play an important role in bringing actors in a field together to develop new framings of the issues, as well as fostering knowledge, shared understanding and dissemination of ideas.

The corporate responsibility movement?

What I have characterised as the corporate responsibility movement has, as has hopefully become apparent, all of the core elements of a social movement. Space constraints prohibit the inclusion of the hundreds of initiatives that the pioneering efforts described in this paper have spawned (though see Waddock 2008a for a much more comprehensive descriptive picture of the corporate responsibility infrastructure that exists at the time of writing). But what the difference makers were able to accomplish through their early efforts—of course along with many, many others, whose work has not been covered here—was to establish the foundational seeds of the infrastructure that has now emerged.

Difference makers accomplished their goals in a wide range of ways. One way was through developing the social investment movement, by reframing the debate about whom corporations serve and how they do so—and broadening that debate to include different stakeholders and the natural environment, using familiar mechanisms (new investment options, indices, shareholder resolutions) and focusing on the issues that mattered to traditional, values-based investors. The difference makers worked by creating markets for data that did not previously exist: for example, the data from social research firms such as KLD and those in the umbrella SiRi organisation. In creating this

---

3 In the interest of full disclosure, I would note that my colleague Samuel Graves and I used the generously granted data from KLD to construct this rating. The ranking has, however, now been taken over by the CRO (Corporate Responsibility Officer) and no longer uses the same methodology that we designed.

data, they recognised a gap in the market that could be filled, finding a new 'opportunity structure' not previously seen by others.

They worked by mobilising the many other people who cared about the same types of issue—social justice, equity, sustainability, and corporate accountability, responsibility and transparency—in various forms of mobilising structures, networks of relatively like-minded individuals who can learn from each other and spread the word about their own best practices. Other approaches involved creating new data on corporate responsibility that could be used in a variety of ways by investors, scholars and others to track corporate performance along lines beyond the strictly financial. Another route was creating coalitions of like-minded parties, or creating forums in which parties with different views could come together in dialogue and learning.

Of course, questions still remain about just how deeply corporate responsibility is embedded in practice and whether this alternative and more expansive view of the purposes and responsibilities of corporations can supplant the dominant economic perspective, with its narrow focus on maximisation of shareholder wealth. But that the movement has had some impact can be little doubted if you consider the fact that the CEOs of two of the world's most successful, intensely competitive, and largest corporations have turned their attention to issues related to corporate responsibility. Lee Scott, CEO of Wal-Mart, a company known for its 'low prices always' and strongly competitive focus on efficiency, has now committed the company to a path of sustainability that encompasses driving sustainability issues not only through its own operations but also throughout its massive supply chain (Scott 2008). And Microsoft founder Bill Gates, whose company is known for its aggressive competitive tactics, called, in January 2008, for a more 'creative capitalism' that 'takes . . . interest in the fortunes of others and ties it to our interest in our own fortunes in ways that help advance both' at the World Economic Forum (Gates 2008).

Further evidence of the inroads that the corporate responsibility movement has made comes from the conservative magazine *The Economist*, which in 2005 issued a special report panning corporate responsibility. In January 2008, however, *The Economist* had to admit that, despite the fact that too few companies are actually doing it well, corporate responsibility is here to stay (Franklin 2008). This paper has explored some of the origins of the wave of corporate responsibility that is with us today. It tries to provide a foundation for suggesting that *The Economist* is correct that corporate responsibility is here to stay—and is only likely to become more important to companies given the growing array of institutions and organisations with an interest in fostering corporate responsibility, the seeds of which can be found in the institutions created in the social movement explored above.

References

Domini, A., and P.D. Kinder (1986) *Ethical Investing* (Reading, MA: Addison-Wesley).

Elkington, J., and J. Hailes (1988) *The Green Consumer Guide* (London: Gollancz).

Franklin, D. (2008) 'Just Good Business', *The Economist* 386.8563 (17 January 2008): 3-6.

Friedman, M. (1970) 'The Social Responsibility of a Business is to Increase its Profits', *New York Times Magazine*, 13 September 1970.

Gates, B. (2008) 'A New Approach to Capitalism in the 21st Century', remarks at the *World Economic Forum*, 24 January 2008; www.computerworlduk.com/management/it-business/it-organisation/opinion/index.cfm?articleid=1120, accessed 15 January 2009.

Hawken, P. (2008) *Blessed Unrest: How the Largest Movement in the World Came into Being and Why No One Saw It Coming* (New York: Viking Press).

Klein, N. (2007) *The Shock Doctrine: The Rise of Disaster Capitalism* (New York: Metropolitan Books).

Lydenberg, S., A.T. Marlin and S. Strub (1986) *Rating America's Corporate Conscience* (Reading, MA: Addison-Wesley).

McAdam, D., J.D. McCarthy and M.N. Zald (1996) 'Introduction: Opportunities, Mobilizing Structures, and Framing Processes—Toward a Synthetic Comparative Perspective on Social Movements', in D. McAdam, J.D. McCarthy and M.N. Zald (eds.), *Comparative Perspectives on Social Movements: Political Opportunities, Mobilizing Structures, and Cultural Framings* (New York: Cambridge University Press): 1-20.

Scott, L. (2008) 'The Company of the Future', remarks by Lee Scott for Wal-Mart US Beginning of Year Meeting, 23 January 2008; walmartstores.com/FactsNews/NewsRoom/7896.aspx, accessed 9 January 2009.

Social Investment Forum (2008) *Executive Summary: 2007 Report on Socially Responsible Investing Trends in the United States* (Washington, DC: Social Investment Forum; www.socialinvest.org/pdf/SRI_Trends_ExecSummary_2007.pdf, accessed 20 June 2008).

Waddock, S. (2008a) 'Building a New Institutional Infrastructure for Corporate Responsibility', *Academy of Management Perspectives* 22.3: 87-108.

—— (2008b) *The Difference Makers: How Social and Institutional Entrepreneurs Created the Corporate Responsibility Movement* (Sheffield, UK: Greenleaf Publishing; www.greenleaf-publishing.com/differencemakers).

Mainstream or Daydream?

The Future for Responsible Investing

Steve Lydenberg
Domini Social Investments, USA

Graham Sinclair
Sinclair & Company, USA

This essay updates a 2002 article entitled 'Envisioning Socially Responsible Investing: A Model for 2006', published in the *Journal of Corporate Citizenship*. Part One highlights developments in the corporate, institutional investor and financial communities, marking the progress of responsible investing and corporate social responsibility since that time. It notes increases by corporations in CSR reporting, both voluntary and mandatory, and in demand for that reporting; a trend by institutional investors toward transparency in proxy voting and the incorporation of social and environmental standards and best practices into investment policies; and the incorporation of social and environmental matters into stock analysis, academic business curricula, and financial professional training.

Part Two raises a number of questions about the possibility of fundamental change in these three worlds. It suggests that, despite various positive developments, fundamental change will take place only when corporations see their contributions to society extending beyond short-term profits to a longer-term view including a cooperative relationship with government; when institutional investors seek broad-based returns to society from all asset classes as part of their fiduciary duties; and when various professional communities recognise that the value of corporations to society can legitimately be measured in terms other than short-term price.

- Responsible investment (RI)
- Pension funds
- Environmental, social and governance (ESG) factors
- Socially responsible investment (SRI)
- Corporate social responsibility (CSR)
- Proxy voting
- Shareholder activism
- Modern portfolio theory

Steven Lydenberg is Chief Investment Officer for Domini Social Investments LLC, and was a co-founder of KLD Research & Analytics. He is co-author of *Investing for Good* (HarperCollins, 1993) and author of *Corporations and the Public Interest: Guiding the Invisible Hand* (Berrett-Koehler, 2005).

✉ Domini Social Investments, 536 Broadway 7th Floor, New York, NY 10012, USA

🖥 slydenberg@domini.com

Graham Sinclair is an ESG architect and sustainability investment strategist. He is involved in modelling investment vehicles in many locations around the world. Graham worked through 2002 in pensions consulting and investment management in South Africa after graduating from Howard College School of Law. He is a Senior Fellow of the Environmental Leadership Program, a professional contributor to the Harvard Kennedy School CSR Initiative, and alum of the WWF One Planet Leaders program. He lectures at Kenan-Flagler Business School.

✉ Sinclair & Company, PO Box 177, Woodstock, VT 05091, USA

🖥 graham.sinclair@sinclairconsult.com

N AUTUMN 2002, AN ARTICLE CALLED 'ENVISIONING SOCIALLY RESPONSIBLE Investing: A Model for 2006', published in the *Journal of Corporate Citizenship*, assessed the state of socially responsible investing. At that time, the author made various predictions about developments that 'may well take place' in the worlds of socially responsible investing within five years (Lydenberg 2002).

That period having passed, some observations on how far in fact socially responsible investing (SRI) has progressed are in order, along with an examination of what developments might reasonably be expected to occur in the next five years. Much progress has been made since 2002, but it is fair to say at this time that responsible investing (RI) is far from mainstream.[1] What it means for RI to be mainstream, what true mainstreaming would look like and what it would take to achieve that goal are among the key questions that this article addresses.

At the heart of this essay lies the question of whether mainstreaming means that responsible investing will become a niche market within a fundamentally unchanged mainstream or, whether it means that the mainstream as a whole will adopt the basic tenets of responsible investing.

Part One of this essay highlights a number of important developments in the *corporate, institutional investor* and *financial communities*, marking the progress of corporate social responsibility (CSR) and RI over the past half dozen years. Part Two raises a number of questions about the possibility of fundamental change in these three worlds. We approach these questions as practitioners of responsible investment, with the various strengths and limitations that this practical experience brings. Academics and economists may well have much to add to our initial observations—in particular by answering in full the questions to which we have here only sketched out various parameters of possible responses. Our hope is that these preliminary observations about where we are in 2009, and where we are headed, can provide a degree of focus to the thinking and offer some direction to the collaborative work that is needed to bring about fundamental change in investment as usual.

Part One: state of responsible investing today

Although a complete account of the progress of responsible investing and corporate responsibility is beyond the scope of this essay, the following observations highlight just how far we have come. As remarkable as the progress has been, however, the changes that have occurred remain primarily superficial and the prospects of fundamental change are still before us.

The corporate community

The 2002 essay predicted, among other things, that most corporations would soon:

▶ 'State clearly and specifically their social and environmental values'

▶ 'Disclose comprehensive data on their actual social and environmental impacts'

▶ 'Adopt specific management practices to integrate these values into their operations'

---

1 The authors have chosen to use the term 'responsible investing' rather than 'socially responsible investing' in this updated article, as it is the term increasingly used in the investment community to identify these practices.

One surprising development in the corporate world is that executives and managers who profess commitment to CSR are no longer viewed as eccentric or misguided. Indeed, in certain regions, notably the United Kingdom and Europe, it is almost as unaccept-able today not to embrace CSR as it was to talk about it publicly half a dozen years ago, a transition mirrored in the changed coverage by the influential business journal *The Economist* from 2005 to 2008.[2] By 2008, while only approximately 4,000 of the world's 75,000 multinational corporations had signed the United Nations Global Compact, 90% of company CEOs participating in the United Nations Global Compact reported doing more than they did five years previously to incorporate ESG (environmental, social and governance) factors into their management strategies (Bielak *et al.* 2007). At the same time, it is fair to say that the actual management of corporations—including the laser-like focus on short-term profits—has yet to change in fundamental ways.

Among the indications of progress in these three areas, the following are particularly noteworthy.

CSR reports and strategies

A tremendous growth has taken place in the number of companies issuing CSR reports and adopting strategies expressly addressing the ESG challenges (Davis and Stephenson 2006). In this sense, both the statements of companies' social and environmental val-ues and their reporting of data in these areas has increasingly become the norm. For example, the Corporate Register found that for the period September 2006 to Decem-ber 2007, 335 of the *Financial Times* Global 500 companies produced CSR reports. An overwhelming majority of European companies filed reports (152 out of 172), while only about half of the North American companies (118 out of 220) did so (The Corporate Reg-ister 2008). In addition, companies are increasingly integrating social and environ-mental reports with traditional financial statements. For one particularly well-integrated example, see the 2006 Annual Report of the French company Schneider Electric.[3]

Government reporting requirements

Governments and regulators increasingly expect, and are beginning to require, CSR reporting. The French government was the first to venture down this road in 2003, when it required publicly traded companies to include some 40 social and environmental indi-cators in their reports to shareholders. More recently, the Swedish government announced in late 2007 that all 55 publicly traded companies in which it holds owner-ship must begin reporting by 2010 on the extensive set of social and environmental indi-cators covered by the Global Reporting Initiatives guidelines.[4] In early 2008, the Chinese government announced that state-owned companies there would be expected to begin reporting on their CSR records (*Ethical Performance* 2008a). In addition, the Argentine capital Buenos Aires has passed legislation requiring large companies head-quartered in that city to publish sustainability reports (*Ethical Performance* 2008b). Since 2006, all listed companies in Malaysia have been required to report on their corporate responsibility policies and programmes to the Malaysian Stock Exchange (Yusof 2006).[5]

---

2 Noteworthy is the change in editorial treatment of the concepts of sustainability and corporate social responsibility from 2005 to 2008. Compare the article entitled 'Corporate Social Responsibility: Just Good Business' (*The Economist* 2008) with 'The Good Company', on this same topic (*The Economist* 2005).

3 www.schneider-electric.com/sites/corporate/en/press/media-library/financial-statements-annual-reports.page, accessed April 2008.

4 www.sweden.gov.se/sb/d/8194/a/93506, accessed 22 March 2008.

5 See also *The Silver Book: Achieving Value through Social Responsibility*, a comprehensive social respon-sibility manual prepared by the Malaysian government for government-linked companies (PCG 2006).

In the UK, the 2006 Companies Act introduced a requirement for public companies to report on social and environmental matters. The Danish Parliament voted in mid-December 2008 to require from 2010 that the 1,100 largest enterprises describe their corporate CSR or socially responsible policies.[6] The United Nations Global Compact increased pressure on its signatories to report regularly on their CSR achievements, removing 394 of approximately 3,775 signatories for inadequate reporting (*Ethical Performance* 2008c).

Interests of investors and consumers

Systematic corporate disclosure on social and environmental issues is increasingly demanded by responsible investors and consumers. For example, in 2008, around 385 institutional investors representing some US$57 trillion had endorsed the Carbon Disclosure Project's call for systematic disclosure of carbon emissions by the 3,000 largest corporations worldwide.[7] Similarly, in September 2007, a coalition of 22 institutional investors representing US$1.5 trillion in assets, and led by Ceres and Environmental Defense, petitioned the US Securities and Exchange Commission to require full corporate climate risk disclosure.[8] One indication of consumer interest in the social and environmental records of companies is the growth of interest in purchasing organic food and clothing as well as fairtrade products. Ethical consuming has taken particularly strong root in the UK, reaching an annual total of some US$65 million in 2007 (Co-operative Bank 2007). In the US, the so-called LOHAS segment (lifestyles of health and sustainability), reached US$209 billion in 2007 (LOHAS 12 Forum 2008). Similarly, the interest in real estate with a 'green' and sustainability theme is increasing around the world. In the US, for example, the 14,000-member US Green Building Council had certified some 1,325 buildings under its LEED (Leadership in Energy and Environmental Design) green building guidelines as of 2008, and has an additional 10,309 buildings undergoing that certification process (US Green Building Council 2008). The 2008 conference attracted over 10,000 delegates.

While these examples illustrate how far CSR and sustainability issues have come since 2002, the trend does not yet demonstrate systematic and comprehensive integration of sustainability and CSR into the daily management decisions and actions of major corporations.

Institutional investors

The 2002 essay also predicted that major institutional investors would soon:

▶ 'Adopt comprehensive voting policies on social, environmental and corporate governance issues including guidelines for voting and the disclosure of actual votes'

▶ 'State publicly the extent to which they incorporate social and environmental issues in their investment practices'

▶ 'Undertake ongoing dialogue among themselves on social and environmental issues, as they already do on corporate governance'

---

6 www.samfundsansvar.dk/sw42800.asp, accessed 12 January 2009.
7 See website of the Carbon Disclosure Project at www.cdproject.net/aboutus.asp, accessed 6 January 2009.
8 See website of the Investor Network on Climate Risk at www.incr.com/NETCOMMUNITY/Page.aspx?pid=397&srcid=330, accessed 24 April 2008.

As with the case of mainstream corporate management, many promising developments have emerged since 2002, most notably in three general areas.

Voting transparency

The expectation that institutional investors should publicly report on their proxy voting is becoming a worldwide phenomenon. In a major development, since 2003, the US Securities and Exchange Commission has required that all mutual funds and money managers publicly report on their proxy voting guidelines and on their proxy voting. This transparency, and the increase in prominence of environmental, social and governance issues, is reflected in the changing behaviour of mutual fund voting on climate change issues (Baue and Cook 2008). In 2006, a Canadian regulation with similar requirements came into effect. In addition, public pension and investment funds have moved significantly on their transparency with respect to proxy voting. Dutch public pension fund PGGM, for example, reports on votes for its 4,000 company portfolios.[9] South Africa's Public Investment Corporation has announced that it will begin publishing its votes at corporate annual meetings (*Global Proxy Watch* 2008). Norway's Government Pension Fund–Global publishes its votes: in 2007, Norge Bank Investment Management (NBIM) voted at a total of 4,202 general meetings, or 89% of the meetings held by portfolio companies.[10]

Pension funds

Governments, especially in Europe, are requiring their national pension funds to adopt social and environmental guidelines for their investments. For example, in 2005 the Norway Pension Fund adopted a series of social, environmental and ethical guidelines that are being gradually implemented.[11] Similarly the Swedish government has directed its national pension funds to consider the implications of social and environmental factors in their investment processes, which resulted in four of the seven so-called 'AP funds' with US$150 billion in assets setting up a Joint Ethical Council in 2007 to monitor environmental and ethical compliance of funds holdings of foreign companies.[12] After the New Zealand government signed an international munitions treaty in Norway in 2008, the US$12 billion New Zealand Superannuation Fund sold US$37 million worth of shares in companies associated with the manufacture of cluster munitions and the manufacture or testing of nuclear explosive devices.[13] State pension funds including Sweden's AP buffer funds, the Norwegian Government Pension Fund and the US$32.7 billion Irish National Pension Reserve Fund (NPRF) divested such munitions firms in 2008 or plan to in 2009. The Danish government introduced new SRI policy initiatives in May 2008 (Kjaer 2008). In the United States, the State of California's Public Employees Retirement System in 2004 launched Green Wave initiative, which imposed environmental guidelines for US$200 million investments in real estate, venture capital and equities (Angelides 2004). In South Africa, the pension funds regulator, the Financial Services Board, in 2007 outlined the principles for good fund governance, with explicit coverage of the approach to responsible investment.[14]

---

9 See PGGM website at www.pggm.nl/About_PGGM/Investments/Responsible_Investment/Voting/Voting.asp#1, accessed 1 May 2008.

10 www.norges-bank.no/templates/report_ _ _ _ 68488.aspx, accessed 12 January 2009.

11 Norge Bank Investment Management has its own Principles for Corporate Governance guidelines on corporate governance, based on OECD and UN Global Compact guidelines, and on the guidelines of the Norwegian government laid down by the Executive Board of Norges Bank (see Syse 2008). In 2007, NBIM published the *Investor Expectations on Children's Rights*.

12 www.ap1.se/en/Asset-management/Ethical-and-environmental-consideration-in-our-investments/Ethical-Council, accessed 12 January 2009.

13 www.responsible-investor.com/home/article/cluster4, accessed 30 December 2008.

14 The Registrar of Pension Funds of the Financial Services Board issued circular PF130 in June 2007; ftp://ftp.fsb.co.za/public/pension/circular/PF1302.pdf, accessed 12 January 2009.

Best practice for responsible investment

Institutional investors are increasingly sharing best practices and collaborating on the incorporation of social and environmental initiatives into their investment practices. Most recently the Principles for Responsible Investment (PRI)[15] aim to connect pension funds and money managers from around the world committed to six principles of responsible investment. The over 400 institutional investors representing around US$18 trillion in assets under management communicate among themselves on their environmental, social and governance policies, coordinate on engagement with companies, and examine best practices for responsible investment.[16]

Despite these encouraging developments, most institutional investors do not yet ordinarily incorporate social and environmental considerations into their decision-making. Nor has investment as usual changed. Investment decisions in the mainstream do not take possible risks or rewards of social and environmental factors into account, except where they incorporate short-term stock price implications.

Financial community

Finally, the 2002 essay also predicted that the mainstream financial, academic and RI communities would take the following steps:

▶ 'Mainstream financial firms will train their analysts to routinely incorporate CSR considerations into securities analysis'

▶ 'The academic community will offer courses and grant degrees in CSR and SRI'

▶ 'The SRI industry will develop quality standards, undertake theoretical research on topics of communal concern, and create a network of issue-specific, niche-market research firms'

A variety of initiatives—substantial in their scope—have emerged since that time within the financial community. Investment vehicles with specific social, environmental or governance (ESG) objectives are increasingly available. The most recent biannual survey of ESG investments in the US, the largest such market, identified US$2.7 trillion in assets under management as of December 2007 (Social Investment Forum 2008). The most recent similar European study in 2006, which covered nine countries, identified €1.6 trillion representing 10–15% of assets under management in those markets. Three noteworthy developments in this area are discussed below.

Enhanced Analytics Initiative

One strategic initiative in the mainstream financial community that broke new ground for RI was the Enhanced Analytics Initiative (EAI) launched in 2004 by asset owners with a long-term perspective. EAI successfully prodded mainstream investment banks to encourage their sell-side analysts to cover environmental, social and governance issues in their stock research. EAI consisted of some 30 institutional investors with approximately US$3 trillion under management committed to allocating 5% of their research budget to investment research, and banking firms whose analysts are judged to present the best coverage of environmental, social and corporate governance factors in their equity analysis (Enhanced Analytics Initiative 2008). In addition, mainstream

---

15 Launched in April 2006 at the New York Stock Exchange under the aegis of the United Nations Global Compact and UN Environment Programme Finance Initiative (see www.unpri.org, accessed 12 January 2009).
16 www.unpri.org, accessed 12 January 2009.

investment houses, such as Société Générale, F&C Asset Management, HBOS, JP Morgan Chase, UBS, Deutsche Bank and Goldman Sachs have in recent years established in-house research teams that conduct analyses for their investor clients on such issues as climate change, renewable energy, water, human rights, nutrition and diversity. In October 2008 the EAI folded into the PRI, while the fallout from the 2008 financial meltdown forced cost cuts at major investment banks including their specialist ESG teams.[17]

Growth in postgraduate courses and centres

Within the academic community, the number of courses offered in MBA programmes continues to grow, albeit slowly. Contributing to this progress has been the growth in the Net Impact network[18] of MBA candidates seeking new curricula that cover ESG themes. The 2007 annual Beyond Grey Pinstripes ranking listed some 60 graduate-level business courses that include CSR components. It ranked Stanford, University of Michigan and York University (Canada) as among those schools with the best offerings.[19] In the US, programmes include Duquesne University's MBA Sustainability programme, Marlboro College's MBA in Managing for Sustainability, and Bainbridge Graduate Institute's MBA in Sustainable Business. In the UK, Nottingham University awards a Corporate Social Responsibility MBA. In Switzerland, HEC Genève offered a masters-level CSR diploma for the first time in 2008, while St Gallen University houses oikos International, a foundation that sponsors up to five PhD fellowships for students pursuing topics of business sustainability, as well as an innovative case sustainability study development programme.

Some progress has also been made in the development of academic resource centres that support the development of RI and CSR. Among those in the United States are the Center for Corporate Citizenship and the Institute for Responsible Investment at Boston College, the University of North Carolina–Chapel Hill Kenan-Flagler Center for Sustainable Enterprise, the Center for the Study of Fiduciary Capitalism at St Mary's College in California, the Center for Responsible Business at the Haas School at the University of California in Berkeley, and the Corporate Social Responsibility Initiative at the Kennedy School of Government at Harvard University. Elsewhere, the European Academy for Business in Society (EABIS) is leading a laboratory on 'Corporate Responsibility and Market Valuation of Financial and Non-financial Performance'[20] while the University of South Africa's Corporate Citizenship Center established a Chair in Responsible Investment in 2007.

These developments are indications of progress, but are still far from representing systematic changes in the philosophy or approach to investing or best practices for investment analysis that currently dominate the financial and academic communities.

---

17 www.responsible-investor.com/home/article/deutsche, accessed 30 December 2008.

18 Net Impact is an organisation including some 10,000 MBAs and post-MBAs in chapters at major business school campuses in North America, Europe and the world (www.netimpact.org, accessed 8 January 2009).

19 Beyond Grey Pinstripes (www.beyondgreypinstripes.org/rankings/index.cfm, accessed 22 March 2008).

20 In cooperation with Cranfield School of Management, University of Lille, University of Bocconi, among others. Umeå University, Sweden, and Maastricht University, The Netherlands, are active in the European Centre for Corporate Engagement (www.corporate-engagement.com/index.php?pageID=1880&n=329#partner_128458, accessed 12 January 2009).

Part Two: key questions about fundamental change

One of the most frequently asked questions about both RI and CSR these days is one of impact. Have RI and CSR brought about fundamental transformations or are they in fact nothing but greenwash and a feel-good palliative that sound good but represent no real change? It is not surprising that this question is arising now. Both RI and CSR are so widely publicised, have received endorsements from such prominent and influential actors, and have aroused such widespread expectations of potential progress toward a better and more sustainable world that indications of real progress will inevitably be demanded.

One disturbing possibility for RI proponents—those of us seeking to influence investment practice to maximise positive externalities and minimise negative externalities—is that this discipline may become just an accepted niche market within the financial community without resulting in any fundamental change. Or similarly, CSR might prove to be no more than a management fad, widely discussed but only sporadically implemented. Both RI and CSR may be studied in academia, but only as curiosities bringing no fundamental change to today's underlying theories of finance and the corporation, and without true legitimisation or institutionalisation of their practices.

Thus, the single most important issue today is whether the 'rules of the game' are going to change. Put differently, the fundamental question is not whether the current financial markets can be used to fix social and environmental problems, although in certain circumstances they certainly can, but whether social and environmental concerns can drive fundamental changes into the current markets, which today create as many social and environmental challenges as they address.

We pose here a set of three specific questions for each of the three communities influential in the marketplace—corporations, institutional investors, and the worlds of finance and academia—that need to be addressed if we are to see such fundamental change (see Appendix). A complete response to each of these questions will require new thinking, vigorous debate and frank discussion. Our brief comments here are intended to point out briefly some of the directions today's thought leaders are currently taking in addressing these questions and to open up a broader forum for more structured and detailed discussions.

Corporations

To understand what it might mean for CSR to be more than a management fad, we pose three questions.

▶ Can the widely accepted definition of the role of the corporation as a short-term profit-maximising machine be changed, and, if so, how?

▶ Will corporations come to recognise that rule-setting by government can enhance their abilities to address social and environmental challenges, and, if so, why?

▶ Can corporations work cooperatively with government to define the relationship between these two powerful forces so that the pursuit of private goods does not undercut the creation of public goods?

Can the widely accepted definition of the role of the corporation as a short-term profit-maximising machine be changed, and, if so, how?
Today's corporate managers are being pulled in two opposite directions. Globalisation and the increasing propagation of the stockowner-centric Anglo-American model of the

corporation drive managers towards relentless profit maximisation. Simultaneously, CSR advocates—including many national governments, the United Nations, academics, and activist non-governmental and international organisations—promote a stakeholder model where managers treat employees, suppliers and local communities and their environment on an equal footing with stockowners. How should corporations best balance the tension between generating short-term profits for stockowners and investing long-term in the full range of their stakeholders?

Unless this question can be resolved in favour of those advocating a stakeholder model of the corporation, corporate management as it is now widely practised is not likely to change fundamentally.[21] This debate is particularly crucial in the United States, where stockowner supremacy has had broad acceptance. A number of efforts to promote a fundamental redefinition of this model are now under way there. For example, Corporation 20/20—a multi-stakeholder collaboration that has proposed six 'principles of corporate redesign'—would build into the definition of the relationship between corporations and society a broader social purpose than profit maximisation. Corporation 20/20 asserts that 'It is no longer enough to ask, "What is the business case for social responsibility?" Now the question must become, "What is the social purpose case for business?" ' (Kelly and White 2007). Similarly, B Corporation, a coalition of small, primarily privately held, for-profit corporations, seeks to brand its members as alternative to the mainstream, setting rigorous standards for their commitments to social and environmental initiatives.[22]

This fundamental shift must also take place on a theoretical level. A number of legal scholars, for example, are evolving new theories of corporate law. Professor Kent Greenfield, in his book *The Failure of Corporate Law*, argues that the laws governing corporations need to be more protective of corporations' various stakeholders and the general public (Greenfield 2006). Similarly, Professors Margaret Blair and Lynn Stout in their article 'Specific Investment and Corporate Law: Explaining Anomalies in Corporate Law', reprinted in collaboration with Corporation 20/20, argue that shareholder primacy is in decline and that an emerging new theory posits that the primary obligation of managers and directors is to recognise 'specific investments' in the company made by various stakeholders and to distribute returns appropriately from those investments to these stakeholders (Blair and Stout 2007).

On a practical level, this means that, as the authors of *Beyond Good Company: Next Generation Corporate Citizenship* argue, a 'transformative change' that moves managers away from the primary focus on stockowners is necessary if CSR is to become fully integrated into for-profit business. If the rules of the game are to change, however, this *redefinition* will need to encompass shifts that are legal, regulatory, theoretical and cultural (Googins *et al.* 2007).

Will corporations come to recognise that rule-setting by government can enhance their abilities to address social and environmental challenges, and, if so, why?

In 2003, Deborah Leipziger published *The Corporate Responsibility Code Book*, which analysed 32 well-established voluntary codes of conduct for corporations (Leipziger 2003). Since then, the rather astounding proliferation of standards, norms, codes and guidelines for best social, environmental and corporate governance practices has continued. Some of these codes of conduct are general in nature, such as those promulgated by the United Nations Global Compact, the Principles for Responsible Investment,

---

21 See Kelly and White 2007 on the Corporation 20/20 website (www.corporation2020.org, accessed 8 April 2008). In addition, the website contains a series of papers addressing various aspects of the question of fundamental corporate redesign.

22 www.bcorporation.net/home.php, accessed 8 April 2008.

the International Labour Organisation, Social Accountability International, the Caux Business Round Table, and others. The International Organisation for Standardisation (ISO) plans to issue its own set of global guidelines for CSR in 2010. Many other sets of standards and principles are industry- or issue-specific. In the past several years, for example, the coffee, tea, cocoa and palm oil industries, as well as the diamond and mineral extraction industries, have developed various codes of conduct specific to their industries.

As these voluntary codes proliferate, it is not surprising that the advantages in terms of legitimacy and simplicity of government's ability to regulate will become increasingly apparent to corporations themselves. In the United States, for example, in 2007 Google called for clearer government regulation of privacy issues on the Internet in the face of public pressure for it to address censorship issues in China; toy manufacturers began lobbying for increased funding for the Consumer Products Safety Commission in the face of increased safety concerns; and the agricultural industry, also facing safety issues in imported foods, called for an increased government monitoring role.

Moreover, the recent crises in the financial markets—which have led to billions of dollars in losses and were catalysed by the overly aggressive practices of unregulated mortgage brokers and the packaging and selling of unregulated asset-backed securities based on these loans by unregulated investment bankers—have reminded the financial services industry that government regulation and backing of the financial markets is essential for assuring their long-term stability.[23]

Both the proliferation of spontaneous voluntary business codes and the periodic resurgence of scandals stemming from the excesses of the unregulated 'invisible hand' of those in the business and financial worlds make it clear that government's role is essential. There may be battles between corporations, government and NGOs over the appropriate circumstances for regulation and the degree of that regulation, but the ground rules will have changed only when corporations are seen fighting for, not against, such oversight.

Can corporations work cooperatively with government to define the relationship between these two powerful forces so that the pursuit of private goods does not undercut the creation of public goods?

During the 1980s, the UK under Margaret Thatcher and US under Ronald Reagan pushed for privatisation and deregulation that in the 1990s led Russia and Eastern Europe to dismantle state ownership of major industries, China to embark on its no less monumental transition towards market-based economies, European governments to privatise multiple sectors of the economy, and US regulators to abandon price controls and monopoly regulation of numerous industries. Advocates of increased worldwide trade cheered these initiatives, while anti-globalisation protestors took to the streets and many pointed with dismay to a weakening of government oversight of a corporate world prone to abuse.

The debate over which goods and services government should provide versus which should be turned over to private enterprise is far from resolved. Which aspects of healthcare should be shouldered by government, the degree to which water utilities should be operated for profit, or who best can provide public transportation, postal services, toll roads and airport maintenance are all topics of ongoing debate. Corporations are not shy about asserting that they can handle such basic services as prisons (e.g. Correction Corporation of America), primary school education (e.g. Edison Alliance) and fighting wars better than governments (see *Corporate Warriors: The Rise of the Privatized Military Industry*, Singer 2003).

---

23 Among many press articles on the need for re-regulation in the financial services industry, see Gavin 2008: C1.

In many senses, the history of the relationship between business and government in the 20th century has been one in which the pendulum has swung from few public goods provided by government to many and back again towards few. Where the pendulum should most appropriately settle will vary from country to country, era to era, and issue to issue. Global capitalism is possible in a world of local values, but it will look different from country to country. Ultimately it is governments' role to decide which goods should be considered public and which private, and where delivery must rely on private–public partnerships. Governments have the power to make these decisions and must have the longer-term vision to use that power in the public interest.

The rules of the game will have changed only when corporations acknowledge both that they should not unduly influence this debate and that government is in fact best qualified to provide many basic services. Corporations must work with government (and each other) to determine the most appropriate balance between public and private. They must understand that refraining from capitalising on narrow self-interest at the expense of the public good—that is, not blindly seeking tax breaks that cripple local governments, subsidies that distort markets, or monopoly protection that short-circuits competition, for example—is often in their broader self-interest. Only then will real change in the concept of corporate responsibility have taken place.

Institutional investors

If RI is to become more than a niche market within the mainstream investment community, a number of fundamental questions will need to be addressed by institutional investors.

▶ Should the goal of investing encompass broad benefits to society as well as short-term, price-based returns, and, if so, in what ways?

▶ Should politics be separated from investment decision-making, and, if so, who is to make this distinction?

▶ Should the practice of responsible investment be applied across asset classes, and, if so, is this practice the same for all classes?

Should the goal of investing encompass broad benefits to society as well as short-term, price-based returns, and, if so, in what ways?
The answer to this question is crucial for institutional investors bound by fiduciary duties. These fiduciaries include the professional managers of pension funds, mutual funds, trust accounts and others entrusted with management of other people's investments, who are bound by the duties of loyalty and care not to use these funds for their own personal benefit. Fiduciaries should not act so as to harm the best interests of trust beneficiaries or clients. Harm, however, is usually defined in terms of narrow financial measures, not broad societal risks. To redefine the scope of these duties, one might ask whether fiduciaries have an obligation not to act in ways that harm their clients when their investment decisions run fundamental risks to society or the environment. Or, more concretely, do fiduciaries have an obligation to consider the implications of investment decisions for global warming, ozone depletion, human rights abuses, the proliferation of weapons of mass destruction, or other widely recognised ills?

Recently, advocates of the concept of the universal investor have argued that the long-term performance of an economy, not of individual stocks, should drive the fiduciary considerations of large institutional investors, since their investments are so diverse as to represent whole economies (Hawley and Williams 2000; Sethi 2005). Moreover, an

October 2005 study by the law firm Freshfields Bruckhaus Deringer concluded that 'ESG [environmental, social and governance] considerations must be taken into account whenever they are relevant to any aspect of the investment strategy (including general economic or political context)' (Freshfields Bruckhaus Deringer 2005).

This approach, however, can fly in the face of what appears to be the common sense rule of investing—buy stocks that will go up. When oil prices are skyrocketing and oil company earnings soaring, oil stocks help the performance of a portfolio, at least in the short term, no matter what your opinion is of the dangers of the global warming to which they contribute. The fundamental question here is whether the increased purchasing power implied by investment decisions (i.e. appreciation in the value of a portfolio) is in the interests of a beneficiary if the world they are living in has become a demonstrably poorer one because of these same decisions. Little connection has currently been successfully drawn between the long-term interests of individual beneficiaries and the social and environmental risks often implicit in the decisions of a powerful investment world.

The rules of the game will have changed when, either through legal redefinition of fiduciary duties or a changed culture of capital stewardship, fiduciaries act on the understanding that the societal implications of their investment decisions, other than simply price performance, are in fact relevant to the interests of their beneficiaries and clients.

Should politics be separated from investment decision-making, and, if so, who is to make this distinction?[24]

One of the tenets of modern portfolio theory (MPT) is that personal preferences—whether idiosyncratic or political—should not be introduced into investment decision-making (Bernstein 2005). Politics and personal preferences make for bad investing for two reasons. First, MPT advocates believe that politics and personal preference produce suboptimal returns because they blind investment professionals to opportunities to profit. Second, as Milton Friedman argues, they believe that competitive capitalism, including the financial markets, 'promotes political freedom because it separates economic power from political power and in this way enables the one to offset the others' (Reich 2008). That is to say, decisions based solely on financial risk/reward returns not only are the best possible investments, but they prevent government from introducing politics into economic management decisions.

The concern of US and European governments over the rise of so-called sovereign wealth funds (SWFs) is based on the fear of what can happen when politics influence investment decisions. SWFs have emerged as a powerful investment force within the past five years as governments, often those flush with revenues from rising oil prices, have set assets aside to fund national pension schemes or simply as a cushion for a 'rainy day'. These funds are large—among them are those of Abu Dhabi (US$600–800 billion as of 2008), Saudi Arabia (US$300 billion) and Norway (US$350 billion)—and effectively give the governments controlling them the potential to exercise political influence by, for example, acquiring companies controlling strategic materials or taking over foreign firms competing with their domestic industries.

Fearing how these assets might be used, the governments of the United States and Europe have asked these funds to disclose their investments and voluntarily agree not to use their funds to gain political advantage through the marketplace, a request to which the governments of Singapore and Abu Dhabi recently agreed (Thomas 2008). In par-

---

24 This section introduces a number of interconnected questions related to modern portfolio theory and the relationship between political opinion and investing. These questions are particularly complicated and need to be amplified and discussed in a broad context which, owing to space considerations, cannot be attempted in this essay.

ticular, efforts have focused on increasing the transparency of these SWFs as they become more active players in the financial markets (B. Davis 2008; Wilson 2008).

In an interesting variation on the *mélange* of politics and investing, several northern European pension funds have in effect deliberately chosen to support certain political beliefs by adopting the strategy of seeking to conform certain of their investments to the spirit of international norms and standards expressed in treaties that their governments have signed. The Norwegian sovereign wealth pension fund has an ethical policy that will not allow investment in companies that manufacture weapons of mass destruction, and as of 2007 had eliminated from consideration some two dozen companies involved with nuclear weapons production. Since these international treaties are clearly the result of political processes, it is hard to argue that these funds are not endorsing political stands. But the politics here is based on transnational consensus—these are international treaties—not narrowly defined national goals (OECD 2007).

The question here is whether narrow political self-interest or dishonesty driven by *greed* can be distinguished from political or personal interests that promote *broad-based societal goods*. While advocates of separating politics from investments are correct in asserting that narrow self-interest, or personal dishonesty driven by greed, can distort economies and compromise honest government and financial markets, they are essentially silent on the issue of whether it is possible for larger questions of public interest to be legitimately incorporated into the investment process. The rules of the game will have changed when investors appreciate that some political views—such as those surrounding the elimination of weapons of mass destruction, the universal applicability of human rights, or the sustainable management of environmental resources—are not strictly personal or local and that they can, properly considered, contribute to the rewards of a responsible investment process.

Should the practice of responsible investment be applied across all asset classes, and, if so, is this practice the same for all classes?

Responsible investing has grown over the past 30 years in a piecemeal fashion. The main focus has been on equities—the stocks of large, publicly traded corporations. The prominence of equities is perhaps accounted for by the emphasis within the early RI movement on changing corporate behaviour in positive ways and the desire of religious investors to avoid companies involved in morally questionable lines of business.

As RI has gained wider acceptance, analogous responsible investment disciplines have begun to emerge for other asset classes as well: social venture capital, 'green' real estate, community-oriented micro-lending. In addition, the growth of what the mainstream investment community refers to as 'alternative' asset classes—in particular hedge funds and private equity firms—has prompted protests from some quarters that these players are heartless and socially detrimental in their relentless pursuit of profits. To counter these concerns, the hedge funds and private equity industry have made some attempts to formulate codes of best practice, including the 2007 Walker Report in the UK[25] and calls from pension funds in Europe in 2008 (P. Davis 2008).

Missing to date from a varied set of efforts to address the different social implications of various investment asset classes is a systematic survey of the particular social and environmental benefits that particular asset classes are particularly suited to create. In 2007, the Institute for Responsible Investment at Boston College published a *Handbook*

---

25 The Walker Report demands private equity transparency. Hundreds of companies owned by private equity funds will have to produce accounts sooner, more often and disclose more information under proposals from banker Sir David Walker. The Walker Report was commissioned by the BVCA, the trade body of the British Private Equity & Venture Capital Association, following widespread criticism by MPs and trade unions of its members' investments (www.walkerworkinggroup.com/?section=10271, accessed 13 May 2008).

on Responsible Investment across Asset Classes in which it pointed out that certain asset classes were naturally suited to address particular social and environmental issues. For example, cash is well suited to address access to capital challenges at a community level; fixed income, because government issues so much of it, is well suited to promote public goods; venture capital is well suited for funding the creation of new business paradigms such as alternative energy or healthcare advances; and public equities are naturally suited to the encouragement of incremental change in large corporations in mature industries (Wood and Hoff 2007). One indication of moves by major institutional investors in this direction came in early 2008 when the US$53 billion French national pension reserve fund announced plans to extend its responsible investment practices to all the asset classes in which it invests (Wheelan 2008).

The landscape of mainstream investment could be said to have truly changed when institutional investors can conceive of responsible investment as a continuum of varying initiatives across asset classes and tailor responsible investments by asset class to be maximally effective in creating positive externalities.

Financial and academic communities

If the financial and academic communities are to fully embrace RI and CSR, they will need to confront a number of substantive questions still unaddressed. Among these are the following.

▶ Should the value of investments be assessed in terms other than stock price, and, if so, what is the yardstick for such measurement?

▶ Should responsible investing be legitimised as a key part of the investment process, and, if so, through what means?

▶ Can individual investors be active enough 'financial citizens' to make responsible investing a reality, and, if not, why not?

Should the value of investments be assessed in terms other than stock price, and, if so, what is the yardstick for such measurement?
Many in today's mainstream financial and academic communities assert that markets are efficient and incorporate all available information into the price of securities. They consequently also believe that the value of an investment to society is adequately measured by its price. Peter Bernstein summarises this argument:

> [T]he best estimates of shadow prices [i.e. intrinsic value] are the prices set in the marketplace, every minute of every trading day. Those prices may not be precisely equal to the shadow prices, but *no other estimate of intrinsic value* is likely to be more accurate than what buyers and sellers agree on in the marketplace (Bernstein 2005, emphasis added).[26]

However, as Robert Monks has pointed out in his recent book *Corpocracy*, classical economics had its roots in moral philosophy. He asks rhetorically, 'Can we judge markets for slaves, prostitution, and weapons of mass destruction solely on whether they are efficient?' But, if efficient markets have no morals, by what other measurement can we value corporations if not these markets? Monks's answer is 'a language of accountability . . . that comprehensively, fairly, and effectively allocates costs and rewards'. Or, as he also puts it, we need a reformed market that will give corporate executives:

---

26 The question of whether or not markets are efficient in establishing price is beyond the scope of this essay. The authors' concern here, however, relates to the question of whether there are limits to what efficiency can reasonably be expected to price.

the tools to measure not just profit and loss, but their impact on the larger society, and then give them a whole symphony of relevant languages—from environmental science to moral philosophy—to talk about what their new measures reveal (Monks 2007).

Monks differs in his approach from those who talk about incorporating social and environmental risks and rewards into the stock prices. Clearly, when these risks are relevant to the efficient pricing of stocks they should be incorporated. But some values (e.g. human life, honesty, peace) are effectively impossible to price; and some risks and rewards—such as climate change, distrust of business, future regulation, equal opportunity employment, open and free media or racial discrimination—can only be valued on time horizons or in contexts that are so far in the future or are so diffuse that their relevance to pricing is difficult, if not impossible, to calculate. Lydenberg has argued elsewhere that separating the measurement of these hard-to-quantify risks and rewards from stock price is in fact desirable and that, in effect, parallel and disconnected measurements of social returns can supplement reporting on financial gains and losses (Lydenberg 2007).

The rules of the game will have changed only when values other than price can be, and are, conveyed in ways that are easily understandable and usable by investors and consumers alike. Finding a language to express these values that is as direct and compelling as price, however, is no simple task. Indeed, it is one with which responsible investors themselves have struggled with only limited success to date.

Should responsible investing be legitimised as a key part of the investment process, and, if so, through what means?

The fact that the financial and academic worlds have been slow to establish standards, training and certification for RI reflects their reluctance to recognise its legitimacy. Conversely, RI will become an integrated part of the discipline of investing when professional credentials are required of those who practise it.

The signs of fundamental change will be clear when they come. Professional organisations such as the CFA Institute, the various trade associations for social investing professionals and accounting bodies will develop curricula, educational courses, and certification processes that spell out the needs of RI clients, the skills required of RI investment professionals, and the standards by which the industry operates. In addition, on the academic front, the standard finance curriculum at business schools will need to accept and contend with the broad responsibilities that financial professionals owe to society.

Some initial steps have been taken in this direction. For example, the CFA Research Foundation published in 2005 a manual on corporate governance (CFA Research Foundation 2005) and in April 2006 a research monograph entitled *The Social Responsibility of the Investment Profession* by Julie Hudson of UBS laying out the conceptual framework of modern portfolio theory within which RI is unfolding (Hudson 2006). In 2005 the World Business Council for Sustainable Development surveyed young investment analysts to understand their viewpoints and training received on ESG integration (WBCSD and UNEP Finance Initiative 2005). In October 2008 the CFA Institute Centre for Financial Market Integrity published a manual for investors interpreting ESG factors in the valuation of publicly traded companies (CFA 2008). Under the aegis of the US Social Investment Forum, the Sustainability Investment Research Analysts Network, established in 2004, has developed a number of informal programmes to serve the professional development of its members. In Australia, the Responsible Investment Association Australasia Certification Program was created in September 2005 to 'promote consistent, standardised disclosure and education about responsible investment' by fund managers and advisers. The Kenan-Flagler Business School at University of North Carolina–Chapel Hill has for three years offered a dedicated course on RI as an

MBA elective.[27] However, academic courses directly addressing responsible investment, as listed in the Beyond Grey Pinstripes 2008 survey, were still few and far between.

While these preliminary steps indicate the direction of future change and point anecdotally to programmes under way, at the current time the financial and academic community could do substantially more to promote the study and professionalisation of this industry. When such initiatives are realised, they will indicate that responsible investing has earned a core position in the financial world.

Can individual investors be active enough 'financial citizens' to make responsible investing a reality, and, if not, why not?
In their 2006 book *The New Capitalists*, Stephen Davis, Jon Lukomnik and David Pitt-Watson postulate a class of 'citizen' investors—'tens of millions of working people who have their pensions and other life savings invested through funds in shares of the world's largest companies'—concerned with 'sustainable, *long-term* corporate performance'. This new class of investor wants to profit 'without shifting expense—such as pollution—to society at large' and will 'compel boards and CEOs to operate in a pragmatic new framework' and 'rebalance power to force different means of resolving problems' (Davis *et al.* 2006).

Is this scenario, which necessitates an active, educated, broad-based class of investors who want a social and environmental as well as a financial return, realistic? What would need to happen for such a class of investors to emerge?

A number of substantial, but conceivable, steps would be necessary to create, at a retail level as opposed to the institutional investor level discussed above, a class of individual citizen investors concerned about the long-term well-being of society. For one thing, the story of responsible investing—its purpose, effectiveness and rewards—would need to be told dramatically and forcefully so that it can be simply communicated and understood. In addition, the execution of responsible investing—the opportunities to put theory into action—would need to be widely available and easy to implement.

The burgeoning world of investments in microfinance provides a glimpse of how these developments might take place. In making small, essentially unsecured loans to the poor and economically disadvantaged who have previously been denied access to the mainstream financial system, microfinance tells success stories that are dramatic and easily understood. A US$100 loan to a fruit vendor in El Salvador may free her from the clutches of loan sharks and help lift her out of abject poverty. Interestingly, the microfinance world is finding ways to allow the small investor to quickly and easily match loans with those in need around the world.[28]

Moreover, the concept of social entrepreneurship is an increasingly popular one across a wide spectrum of actors who are working to bridge the gap between non-profit and for-profit organisations and are blurring the traditional line between the two. For example, in the venture capital field the success of such organisations as Social Venture Network illustrates this trend.[29]

The successful pioneering steps that the worlds of microfinance and social entrepreneurship have made will need to be brought to scale and applied in other asset classes such as equities, real estate and fixed income. For all these asset classes, investors will need to have quick and easy access to the social and environmental stories that are implied by their choices—whether it is through websites, newsletters, reports, labels, the press, word of mouth or other means. We are still a long way from providing the simplicity and clarity that will encourage the development of such a class of citizen

---

27 www.kenan-flagler.unc.edu/assets/includes/popup.cfm?id=722, accessed 12 January 2009.
28 For example, the microfinance organisation Kiva (www.kiva.org, accessed 8 January 2009).
29 www.svn.org/, accessed 8 January 2009.

investors. But we will know the rules of the game have changed when it is as fashionable to talk about the social returns of one's investments as it is to tell tales of making a killing in the market.

The implications of fundamental change

These nine questions imply a number of radical departures from today's norms in the financial and corporate worlds. In the broadest sense, they imply what could be characterised as a reconceptualisation of the ways in which government, corporations, non-governmental and quasi-governmental organisations and individuals collaborate in managing the interplay between markets and public policy.

Do we really want to tinker with how this balance is currently achieved? After all, as the saying goes, 'if it ain't broke, don't fix it'.

One of the implications of the full integration of CSR and RI into the mainstream would be to create a greater, more cooperative role for for-profit corporations in helping to achieve basic social and environmental goals. For those who believe that corporations are already too powerful in this world, already have too much influence, this may appear to be a dangerous step. For them, the role of government, not corporations, should be strengthened.[30]

Put differently, imagining CSR and RI fully integrated into the mainstream necessitates imagining a system of governance different from the traditional one where corporations' relationship to society is defined primarily through legislation, regulation or state ownership.

For-profit corporations are certainly self-interested creatures who will not hesitate to act in their own interests—and at the expense of the public good—when left to their own devices. If CSR and SRI are no more than a sheep's clothing that will allow the uncontrolled reign of multinational corporations in the halls of government, then bringing these practices into the mainstream is an unwise move that will lead to nothing but abuse and harm. Those who wish to address these dangers through traditional governance methods advocate abandoning talk of CSR and RI and instead propose clearly separating public goods and private enterprise onto two sides of a field—with government on the side of providing public goods and corporations set free on the other to pursue private gains. This view maintains that the often diverging interests and antagonistic relationships between these two players should be acknowledged, and a strong fence (i.e. regulation, legislation, ownership control) should be erected between them to make, as the proverb suggests, good neighbours.

However, as should be apparent from the above, the mainstreaming of RI and CSR implies a blurring of the line between government and for-profit corporations. It envisions a cooperative, rather than antagonistic, relationship between the two. Under this model, government and corporations cooperatively approach goods where they lie on a continuum from public to private, deciding in each case which party should play a dominant or subordinate role in providing them. The answer to the question of balance between the public and private—between the regulatory and the voluntary—will vary depending on the goods in question, the history and culture in which the question arises, and the relative capabilities of government and business at that time and place. The goal of government and business under this scenario, however, should be identical—the building of a stable and valuable structure on this field with long-term sustainability.

It is tempting to view these scenarios as mutually exclusive: either companies must be set free to maximise their profits by any legal means or government and corporations must form partnerships to provide societal goods.

---

30 For an articulate statement of this position, see Reich 2008.

It is fair to say, however, that in the view of many advocates of an increased role for RI and CSR both lines should be pursued simultaneously, and that perhaps a third party—the non-governmental organisation (NGO) and quasi-governmental organisations—should play a prominent role in this dynamic. There will be circumstances where government must act clearly and definitely on a national or global level—for example, workplace safety or ozone depletion—and voluntary, market-driven initiatives are not to be trusted. There will be circumstances where cooperative engagement, rather than legislation, is a viable option: for example, energy efficiency and marketing to those at the bottom of the economic pyramid. There will be times when NGOs and quasi-governmental organisations play an invaluable role in prompting both business and government to greater action: for example, on labour standards in developing countries or corruption and collusion between government and business. Further questions regarding the governance, professionalism and competing agendas of non-governmental organisations and international organisations are important to consider, but beyond the scope of this paper.

Under many circumstances, particularly where actions impose costs on consumers or cut into company profits, corporations need government to create a level playing field, and voluntary initiatives can proceed only haltingly. Under other circumstances, particularly where actions create cost savings for consumers or increase company profits, corporations can be set free to compete in ways that create social and environmental benefits. In some circumstances, both avenues will be pursued simultaneously. For example, to promote the sale of energy-efficient home appliances that may initially cost consumers more but are cost savers in the long run, governments can mandate labels that allow customers to make this calculation and set corporations free to compete voluntarily on these lines. Moreover, government's ability to create and support markets through tax incentives and other subsidies can direct markets through a kind of soft regulation.

In essence, those who favour mainstreaming RI and CSR believe such a flexible and cooperative system is realistic. The relatively strong government support for CSR from national governments in Europe (as opposed to the relatively weak support from US federal government to date) reflects in many ways the historically closer cooperation between government and corporations in that region and the knowledge that government can control corporate behaviour by nationalising companies when regulation fails (for example, the recent nationalisation of Northern Rock bank by the UK government or the nationalisation of financially troubled banks by Scandinavian governments in the 1990s) (Perry 2008). Those who believe efforts to promote RI and CSR have already gone too far and should be dismantled see corporations and governments as fundamentally antagonistic and do not believe that cooperative models can or should be built. Those who believe RI and CSR can and should be pushed further into the mainstream believe these cooperative models are useful and achievable. The truth probably lies between these poles, and will vary according to circumstances.

The above nine questions in effect suggest that a form of tripartite governance (government, corporations, NGOs) can be a useful one, but that it changes the rules of the current games of business and finance. Although its details may still be obscured in the mists of the future and its practicality is still untested, it is possible to see its broad outlines. The promise it offers is a means of harnessing the creative powers of for-profit corporations in ways that complement, not undercut, government's ability to create public goods. Whether we can find our way through those mists remains to be seen. Undoubtedly, however, this will require concerted and cooperative efforts by government, corporations, non-profit institutions and quasi-governmental bodies if we are to proceed down this path. Without these cooperative efforts, fundamental change is unlikely.

References

Angelides, P. (2004) Press Release, California State Treasurer Phil Angelides; www.treasurer.ca.gov/greenwave/020304_enviro.pdf, accessed 22 March 2008.

Baue, B., and J. Cook (2008) *Mutual Funds and Climate Change: Opposition to Climate Change Resolutions Begins to Thaw* (Boston, MA: Ceres).

Bernstein, P.L. (2005) *Capital Ideas: The Improbable Origins of Modern Wall Street* (Hoboken, NJ: John Wiley).

Bielak, D., S.M.J. Bonini and J.M. Oppenheim (2007) 'CEOs Surveyed Representing 230 Organizations in Private/Public, State-Owned and NGOs', *McKinsey Quarterly*, October 2007: 391.

Blair, M., and L. Stout (2007) 'Specific Investment and Corporate Law: Explaining Anomalies in Corporate Law'; www.corporation2020.org/SummitPaperSeries.pdf, accessed 22 March 2008.

CFA Institute Centre for Financial Market Integrity (2008) *Environmental, Social, and Governance Factors at Listed Companies: A Manual for Investors* (Charlottesville, VA: CFA Institute Centre Publications; www.cfainstitute.org/centre): 1-35.

CFA Research Foundation (2005) *The Corporate Governance of Listed Companies: A Manual for Investors* (Charlottesville, VA: CFA Institute Centre for Financial Market Integrity).

The Co-operative Bank (2007) 'Ethical Consumerism Report 2007', *Ethical Consumer*, www.ethicalconsumer.org/ethicalconsumerismreport.htm, accessed 6 January 2009.

The Corporate Register (2008) *The Corporate Climate Communications Report 2007* (London: The Corporate Register): 12.

Davis, B. (2008) 'OECD addresses issue of sovereign-wealth funds', *Wall Street Journal*, 9 April 2008; online.wsj.com/article/SB120768750431299087.html?mod=sphere_ts&mod=sphere_wd, accessed 13 May 2008.

Davis, I., and E. Stephenson (2006) 'Ten Trends to Watch in 2006: Macroeconomic Factors, Environmental and Social Issues', *McKinsey Quarterly*, 18 January 2006; www.mckinseyquarterly.com/strategy/strategy_in_practice/ten_trends_to_watch_in_2006_1734, accessed 31 March 2009.

Davis, P. (2008) 'Pensions demand more liquidity and transparency', *Financial News Online*, 12 May 2008; www.efinancialnews.com/homepage/specialfeatures/2350605250/content/2450611753, accessed 13 May 2008).

Davis, S., J. Lukomnik and D. Pitt-Watson (2006) *The New Capitalists: How Citizens are Reshaping the Corporate Agenda* (Cambridge, MA: Harvard Business School Press): xi-xvii.

The Economist (2005) 'The Good Company', *The Economist*, 20 January 2005.

—— (2008) 'Corporate Social Responsibility: Just Good Business', *The Economist*, 17 January 2008.

Enhanced Analytics Initiative (2008) Press Release, 29 January 2008; www.enhancedanalytics.com/portal/Library/Documents/EAI/NEWS/en_LIB05352.pdf, accessed 12 January 2009.

Ethical Performance (2008a) 'Chinese officials issue guidelines', *Ethical Performance* 9.9; www.ethicalperformance.com/europeamericas/articleView.php?articleID=4924, accessed 31 March 2009.

—— (2008b) 'City of 13 million legislates on mandatory reporting', *Ethical Performance* 9.11; www.ethicalperformance.com/europeamericas/articleView.php?articleID=5018, accessed 31 March 2009.

—— (2008c) 'Global Compact removes 400 "free rider" companies', *Ethical Performance* 9.9; www.ethicalperformance.com/europeamericas/articleView.php?articleID=4914, accessed 31 March 2009.

—— (2008d) 'Danish fund follows trend on cluster bomb divestment', *Ethical Performance* 9.11; www.ethicalperformance.com/europeamericas/articleView.php?articleID=5020, accessed 31 March 2009.

Freshfields Bruckhaus Deringer (2005) 'A Legal Framework for the Integration of Environmental, Social and Governance Issues into Institutional Investment', written for the Asset Management Working Group of the UNEP Finance Initiative; www.unepfi.org/fileadmin/documents/freshfields_legal_resp_20051123.pdf, accessed 1 May 2008.

Gavin, R. (2008) 'Regulation pendulum swinging the other way', *Boston Globe*, 1 April 2008: C1.

Global Proxy Watch (2008) *Global Proxy Watch* 12.8 (22 February 2008): 1.

Googins, B.K., P.H. Mervis and S.A. Rochlin (2007) *Beyond Good Company: Next Generation Corporate Citizenship* (New York: Palgrave Macmillan).

Greenfield, K. (2006) *The Failure of Corporate Law: Fundamental Flaws and Progressive Possibilities* (Chicago: University of Chicago Press).

Hawley, J.P., and A.T. Williams (2000) *The Rise of Fiduciary Capitalism: How Institutional Investors Can Make Corporate America More Democratic* (Philadelphia, PA: University of Pennsylvania Press).

Hudson, J. (2006) *The Social Responsibility of the Investment Profession* (CFA Monograph; Charlottesville, VA: Research Foundation of CFA Institute; www.cfapubs.org/doi/abs/10.2470/rf.v2006.n3.4251, accessed 12 January 2009).

Kelly, M., and A. White (2007) 'Corporate Design: The Missing Business and Public Policy Issue of Our Time', Corporation 20/20; www.corporation2020.org, accessed 8 April 2008.

Kjaer, V. (2008) 'Denmark: When a Country Aligns on ESG Factors', at the *IMN Scandinavian Summit*, Copenhagen, 6–7 May 2008.

Leipziger, D. (2003) *The Corporate Responsibility Code Book* (Sheffield, UK: Greenleaf Publishing).

LOHAS 12 Forum (2008) Press Release, March 2008; www.lohas.com/content/LOHAS12MarchLeadRelease.pdf, accessed 1 May 2008.

Lydenberg, S. (2002) 'Envisioning Socially Responsible Investing: A Model for 2006', *Journal of Corporate Citizenship* 7 (Autumn 2002): 57-77.

—— (2007) 'Long-Term Investing: A Proposal for How to Define and Implement Long-Term Investing', Corporation 20/20 Paper Series on Corporate Design; www.corporation2020.org/SummitPaperSeries.pdf, accessed 18 April 2008.

Monks, R.A.G. (2007) *Corpocracy: How CEOs and the Business Roundtable Highjacked the World's Greatest Wealth Machine and How to Get It Back* (Hoboken, NJ: John Wiley): 22-23, 196, 217.

OECD (2007) *OECD Roundtable on Corporate Responsibility: The OECD Guidelines for Multinational Enterprises and the Financial Sector: Recent Trends and Regulatory Implications in Socially Responsible Investment for Pension Funds* (Paris: OECD).

PCG (2006) 'The Silver Book: Achieving Value through Social Responsibility'; www.pcg.gov.my/PDF/Silver%20booklet%20cover.pdf, accessed 18 May 2008.

Perry, J. (2008) 'Swedish Solution: A Bank-Crisis Plan That Worked', *Wall Street Journal*, 7 April 2008: A2.

Reich, R. (2008) *Supercapitalism: The Transformation of Business, Democracy and Everyday Life* (New York: Borzoi Books): frontispiece.

Sethi, S.P. (2005) 'Investing in Socially Responsible Companies is a Must for Public Pension Funds', *Journal of Business Ethics* 56: 99-129.

Singer, P.W. (2003) *Corporate Warriors: The Rise of the Privatized Military Industry* (Ithaca, NY: Cornell University Press).

Social Investment Forum (2008) *Report on Socially Responsible Investing Trends in the United States 2007* (Washington, DC: Social Investment Forum).

Syse, H. (2008) 'Reflections on the Norwegian Experience with Active Ownership', presentation at the *IMN Scandinavian Summit*, Copenhagen, 7 May 2008.

Thomas, L., Jr (2008) 'Sovereign Funds Weigh Hostile Receptions', *International Herald Tribune*, 2 April 2008: 13.

US Green Building Council (2008) 'Green Building Facts'; www.usgbc.org/ShowFile.aspx?DocumentID=3340, accessed 22 March 2008.

WBCSD (World Business Council for Sustainable Development) and UNEP Finance Initiative (2005) 'Generation Lost: Young Financial Analysts and Environmental, Social and Governance Issues'; www.wbcsd.org/web/publications/ymt-perspectives.pdf, accessed 13 May 2008.

Wheelan, H. (2008) 'France's FRR plots SRI review for all asset classes', *Responsible Investor*, 15 April 2008; www.responsible-investor.com/home/article/frr, accessed 16 April 2008.

Wilson, H. (2008) 'Sovereign funds get call for rise in transparency', *Wall Street Journal Europe*, 9 May 2008; online.wsj.com/article/SB121028369406478821.html, accessed 13 May 2008.

Wood, D., and B. Hoff (2007) *A Handbook for Responsible Investment Across Asset Class* (Boston, MA: Boston College Center for Corporate Citizenship).

Yusof, Y.M. (2006) 'Bursa Malaysia's CSR Framework for Malaysian PLCs'; www.klse.com.my/website/bm/about_us/the_organisation/csr/downloads/csr_framework_slides.pdf, accessed 17 May 2008.

Appendix: nine questions on the future of responsible investment

Corporations

1. Can the widely accepted definition of the role of the corporation as a short-term profit maximising machine be changed, and, if so, how?

2. Will corporations come to recognise that rule-setting by government can enhance their abilities to address social and environmental challenges, and, if so, why?

3. Can corporations work cooperatively with government to define the relationship between these two powerful forces so that the pursuit of private goods does not undercut the creation of public goods?

Institutional investors

1. Should the goal of investing encompass broad benefits to society as well as short-term, price-based returns, and if so, in what ways?

2. Should politics be separated from investment decision-making, and, if so, who is to make this distinction?

3. Should the practice of responsible investment be applied across asset classes, and, if so, is this practice the same for all classes?

Financial and academic communities

1. Should the value of investments be assessed in terms other than stock price, and, if so, what is the yardstick for such measurement?

2. Should responsible investing be legitimised as a key part of the investment process, and, if so, through what means?

3. Can individual investors be active enough 'financial citizens' to make responsible investing a reality, and, if not, why not?

The Corporate Responsibility Movement

Five Years of Global Corporate Responsibility
Analysis from Lifeworth, 2001–2005

JEM BENDELL

with

Désirée Abrahams, Mark Bendell, Tim Concannon, Paul Gibbons,
Kate Ives, Kate Kearins, John Manoochehri, Jeremy Moon, Jules Peck,
Rupesh Shah, Shilpa Shah, Wayne Visser and Mark Young

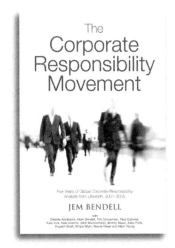

387 + viii pp   234 × 156 mm   Paperback   ISBN 9781906093181   List price: £80.00/€120.00/US$150.00   Published March 2009

Corporate social responsibility is now an established agenda for large companies, with a new profession emerging that engages in the social and environmental contribution of business. How has this agenda emerged over time? What were the key events and actors? How has this new 'movement' of committed individuals been taking shape around the globe? Insights into these questions come from a review of the first half of the first decade of the 21st century. **The Corporate Responsibility Movement** compiles Lifeworth's highly praised Annual Reviews of Corporate Responsibility from 2001 to 2005. It is introduced with a new overview by the lead author of those reviews, Dr Jem Bendell, in a piece that examines the trajectory of a new social movement in and around business. At a time of searching questions about the future of finance, Dr Bendell argues that a new concept of 'capital democracy' is emerging from within the community of people working towards corporate responsibility, which could be mainstreamed as a socially and environmentally enhanced system of economy. He calls on professionals, researchers and policy-makers to embrace an ambitious agenda for corporate responsibility and develop greater insight into acting together as a movement for change. This book is an essential resource for business libraries, recording, analysing and contextualising some of the key events, issues and trends during this historic period in the development of the corporation.

> "Jem Bendell's latest book is a timely reflection on the cultural and behavioural drivers that can help to transform the future role and purpose of business. The financial crisis has brought us to an economic crossroads. However, it also offers a unique window for a collective reshaping of the relationship between business, government and society. This book offers a range of challenging insights to those — especially corporate responsibility managers and executives — seeking to engage in that change process within their organisations."
>
> **Simon Pickard, Director General, European Academy of Business in Society**

> "This is a fantastic resource for libraries that will help readers explore the emergence of contemporary corporate responsibility."
>
> **Andrew Crane, George R. Gardiner Professor of Business Ethics,
> Schulich School of Business**

Greenleaf
PUBLISHING

ORDER ONLINE AND SAVE 10%

More details and a sample excerpt from the Introduction available at www.greenleaf-publishing.com/crmovement

What the Papers Say: Trends in Sustainability

A Comparative Analysis of 115 Leading National Newspapers Worldwide

Ralf Barkemeyer, Frank Figge and Diane Holt
Queen's University Management School, UK

Tobias Hahn
Euromed Marseille School of Management, France

● Corporate
citizenship

● Corporate social
responsibility

● Sustainability

● Sustainable
development

● Corporate
accountability

● Triple bottom
line

● Media
representation

● Text mining

● Newspaper
analysis

● Document
frequencies

This paper presents an overview of the results of a longitudinal analysis of the coverage of sustainability-related concepts in 115 leading national newspapers worldwide between January 1990 and July 2008—covering approximately 20,500,000 articles in 340,000 newspaper issues in 39 countries. On a global level, 'sustainable development' and 'corporate social responsibility' seem to have reached the mainstream public arena, whereas the coverage of 'corporate citizenship' and 'corporate sustainability' remains marginal. The increase in sustainability-related media coverage since 1990 largely seems to be of an incremental nature, rather than clearly associated with specific events. Only very few truly global events can be identified that triggered a substantial amount of media coverage globally. Furthermore, marked regional and national differences in the coverage of sustainability-related concepts can be identified.

Ralf Barkemeyer is a lecturer in management and sustainability at Queen's University Management School, Belfast. He mainly focuses on the interface of business, environment and society. In particular, his main research interests are contemporary CSR-related policies and practices, the relationship of CSR and international development, and value-oriented approaches to measuring and managing corporate sustainability.

✉ Queen's University Management School, Queen's University Belfast, 25 University Square, Belfast BT7 1NN, Northern Ireland, UK

🖥 r.barkemeyer@qub.ac.uk

⊕ qub.ac.uk/mgt

Professor **Frank Figge** holds the Chair of Management and Sustainability at Queen's University Management School. His main research interests are corporate social responsibility, sustainable business, sustainable finance and valuation, social and environmental accounting, stakeholder management and the economics and management of diversity.

✉ Queen's University Management School, Queen's University Belfast, 25 University Square, Belfast BT7 1NN, Northern Ireland, UK

🖥 f.figge@qub.ac.uk

Dr **Tobias Hahn** is an associate professor for corporate sustainability, corporate social responsibility, and environmental management at Euromed Marseille School of Management. He holds a master's degree in environmental science and a PhD in economics and social science. His major research interests include the management and measurement of corporate sustainability and the analysis of stakeholder behaviour.

✉ Euromed Marseille School of Management, Domaine de Luminy – BP 921, 13 288 Marseille cedex 9, France

🖥 tobias.hahn@euromed-management.com

⊕ www.euromed-management.com

Dr **Diane Holt** joined Queen's University Management School in May 2007 as a lecturer in management and sustainability as part of the University's major initiative in sustainability. Her current research interests include green supply chain management, sustainable development in the developing world, environmental marketing and communications.

✉ Queen's University Management School, Queen's University Belfast, 25 University Square, Belfast BT7 1NN, Northern Ireland, UK

🖥 d.holt@qub.ac.uk

N RECENT YEARS, CONCEPTS SUCH AS SUSTAINABLE DEVELOPMENT, corporate citizenship or corporate social responsibility have received an increasing amount of attention in academia. Figure 1 depicts the combined frequency of the terms 'corporate citizenship' and 'corporate social responsibility' in various academic databases between the years 1990 and 2007 (indexed by average 1990–1994). A marked rise in frequency, ranging between factors of 12 (Science Direct) and 45 (Cambridge Scientific Abstracts) can be identified which documents the unprecedented popularity of this current mode of corporate responsibility characterised by the above terms.[1]

However, in order to unfold momentum, these concepts and related issues will have to move beyond academia, and have to make an impact in the public arena. Have these concepts and related issues actually succeeded in reaching mainstream public awareness and opinion? Or have they rather—at least to a certain extent—remained *artificial* concepts that are confined to academia and the CSR departments of large multinational firms, while failing to reach the broader public?

The aim of this paper is to identify key trends in sustainability, and to analyse how media representation of concepts and issues has evolved over time in different countries and regions. Consequently, it is expected to identify priorities and trade-offs within the broad area of sustainability, and therefore to get a clearer understanding of how broad concepts such as sustainable development, sustainability, corporate citizenship and corporate social responsibility are shaped and interpreted by the broader public in different countries and regions. The results of the analysis are largely unequivocal. In general, a significant increase in the media coverage of (corporate) sustainability-related concepts since 1990 can be identified. This increase seems to be of an incremental nature, rather than distinctly associated with a certain number of events. Only very few truly global events can be identified that triggered a substantial amount of media coverage globally. Among these are the Earth Summits in Rio de Janeiro 1992, New York 1997 and Johannesburg 2002, the Conference of the Parties to UNFCCC (UN Framework Convention on Climate Change) in Kyoto, 1997, and possibly the Enron scandal or the awarding of the Nobel Peace Price to Al Gore and the IPCC (Intergovernmental Panel on Climate Change). However, a common trait of most events is that coverage decreased in the aftermath of the events back to similar levels to those that had been measured prior to these events. Only the 2002 Johannesburg Summit might have altered the debate around sustainability and triggered higher, and sustained, levels of media coverage.

The remainder of this paper is structured as follows: first, a brief overview of the relationship between media coverage as an indicator of public awareness and its role in the political agenda-setting process as well as implications for other actors (such as corporate actors) is provided. In particular, findings from international and comparative policy analysis are presented and refined. Subsequently, the methodology applied for the analysis is described. In the next part, some of the key results of the analysis are presented. The analysis comprises: (a) an overview of the evolution of core concepts in sustainability worldwide; and (b) a comparative analysis of leading national UK, US and South African newspapers as well as a selection from various South-East Asian countries, covering various concepts in the field of (corporate) sustainability. The paper concludes with a discussion of the results and a suggested future research agenda.

---

1 Taking into account the fact that, between 1990 and 2007, the size of respective databases and available publications has also risen significantly, a factor of between 4 (Science Direct) and 16 (Cambridge Scientific Abstracts) can still be identified.

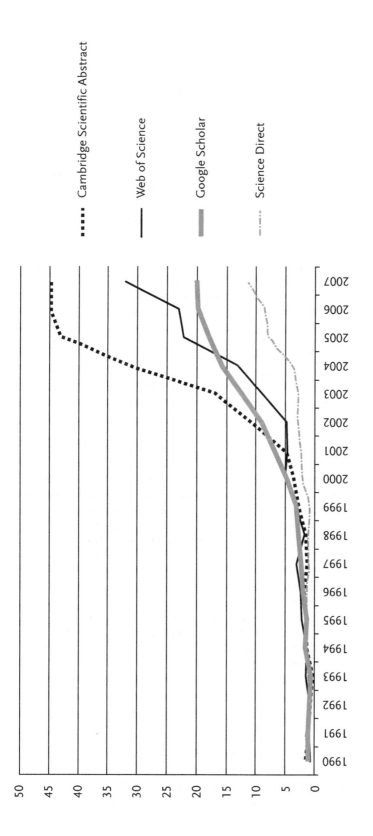

······· Cambridge Scientific Abstract

——— Web of Science

▬▬▬ Google Scholar

–··–·· Science Direct

Figure 1 COMBINED FREQUENCY OF TERMS 'CORPORATE CITIZENSHIP' AND 'CORPORATE SOCIAL RESPONSIBILITY'

Source: various databases 1990–2007

Corporate responsibility, the media and the public

In this paper it is argued that the success of the current wave of new (and more concil-iatory) modes of governance and agency beyond the state, both at a policy level in the form of global governance, and at a corporate level in the form of corporate social respon-sibility or corporate citizenship, will depend heavily on broader public awareness and participation.

Banerjee et al. (2003) identify 'public concern' as one of three key factors external to the company affecting the extent and nature of 'corporate environmentalism', besides 'regulatory forces' and 'competitive advantage'. In addition, it should be noted that both of the latter in turn can be assumed to be affected by the level of public concern. Natu-rally, the broader public would be expected to form an integral element in conceptions of business responsibility towards the broader public as well as in policy-level responses in the field of sustainable development. For example, it has been suggested that the con-tent and intensity of public opinion has been more influential for the development of national environmental policy in the United States than the creation of national-level institutions for environmental policy (Vogel 1993).

The level of media coverage of certain developments in the field of sustainable devel-opment can serve as one indicator of public awareness and opinion. However, it should be noted that media coverage may form one necessary, but not a sufficient precondition for respective (corporate) responses in this field. Only very few cases can be identified in which high levels of international media coverage might have triggered an instant response by large multinational companies such as in the Brent Spar case (Zygli-dopoulos 2002). Instead, a number of factors commonly mediate and moderate (Baron and Kenny 1986) the relationship between the public agenda and the policy agenda (Jänicke 1996, 2002; Weidner 2002; Weidner and Jänicke 2002a) or the corporate agenda (Banerjee et al. 2003). Furthermore, corporate activities or policy processes do not necessarily need to be connected to the extent of media coverage. On a policy level, the first German wave of environmental institutionalisation in the 1970s took place prior to any notable media pressure. Likewise, on a corporate level, a long-standing tradition of 'ethical' and 'socially responsible' companies can be identified in most parts of the world that dates back far beyond the current generation of corporate citizenship or cor-porate social responsibility. Furthermore, in particular in non-OECD countries, in both environmental policy and corporate environmental practice global diffusion processes have been identified that were triggered by a range of transnational rather than national actors and processes (Chudnovsky and Lopez 1999; Jänicke et al. 2000; Weidner 2002; Weidner and Jänicke 2002b; Tews et al. 2003).

Nonetheless, a general relationship between media coverage and corporate social and environmental performance—albeit moderated and mediated by a number of factors—can be assumed. In the context of public agenda setting, two general functions can be attributed to the media: first, to merely transmit or condense 'public opinion'; and, sec-ond, to actively shape the public agenda (for examples in the context of sustainable devel-opment see Lewis 2000; Jänicke 2002: 14; Valenti 2003). Norris (2001) assigns three distinct functions to the media in a representative democracy: the functions of (a) a civic forum; (b) a mobilising agent; and (c) a watchdog. Regarding all three functions, an analysis of media coverage in a given societal context should, at least to a certain extent, allow us to shed light on the level of public awareness or attention regarding specific developments, issues and priorities in this specific national context.

It should be noted that the relationship between 'public opinion' and the extent and nature of media coverage is also mediated and moderated by a number of variables, in turn affecting all of the above functions that can be attributed to the media. Two such variables can be expected to be the ownership structure of a newspaper and its target audience. Another factor might be the changed role of newspapers in society alongside recent advances in information technology and related 'media malaise' theories (for an overview see Norris 2001). In their qualitative analysis of two German and two Dutch newspapers regarding the coverage of two specific EU policies, Bijsmans and Altides (2007) show that newspaper coverage in different countries can differ significantly. Similarly, Brossard *et al.* (2004) assert that significant differences between French and US-based newspapers existed regarding the coverage of climate change-related news stories (Brossard *et al.* 2004). Taking the example of newspaper coverage of anthropogenic climate change in the United States and United Kingdom, Boykoff (2007) shows how different regional backgrounds, as well as the journalistic norm of balanced reporting influence, and are influenced by the framing and representation of a certain issue.

The results of the longitudinal newspaper analysis reported in the following sections will shed light on global-level awareness and perceptions regarding various conceptions of sustainability and corporate responsibility, as well as specific development in different national contexts between the years 1990 and 2008.

Methodology

In this section, the methodology applied in the study is described and justified, focusing on: (a) the research design; (b) sample selection; (c) text mining and transformation; (d) data analysis; and (e) limitations of this approach.

Research design

This study comprises a longitudinal analysis of the coverage of sustainability-related concepts in 115 leading national newspapers based in 39 countries. A keyword search of key terms related to pivotal concepts within the field of sustainability with particular focus on corporate responsibility has been carried out, covering approximately 20,500,000 articles in 342,000 newspaper issues. The technique that has been applied can be described as text (data) mining (Hearst 1997, 1999; Manning and Schütze 2002) or knowledge discovery from textual databases (Feldman and Dagan 1995). It is thus based on the broader field of data mining from knowledge discovery in databases (KDD) (Fayyad *et al.* 1996; Tan 1999).

Text mining refers to the process of generating patterns or knowledge from unstructured or semi-structured text (Tan 1999; Feldman and Sanger 2007). In this study, one of the most basic forms of text mining, the search for specific words contained in a sample of documents (Lent *et al.* 1997), is carried out. The document frequency of pivotal terms related to the field of sustainability and corporate responsibility is identified in the above-mentioned newspaper sample and subsequently analysed longitudinally and on a regional level.

Sample selection

In total, the sample consists of approximately 20,500,000 articles from 342,000 issues between January 1990 and July 2008 of leading national newspapers based in 39 countries. In those cases in which newspapers were not accessible through the databases over the full period of analysis, they were included in the sample as from the first full month they became available. Selection criteria were, among others, circulation, area of circulation and, if possible, private ownership. In terms of area of circulation, we aimed for newspapers that were not predominantly local or regional in scope and therefore at least to a certain extent reflected the national public agenda. One important aim in the selection process was to create a sample that was as geographically diverse as possible, especially with regard to non-OECD countries. Therefore, the number of newspapers from countries such as the United States, the UK or Germany, in which data availability is less of a factor, has been limited to a maximum of eight, in order to minimise the bias towards these countries, and to arrive at a varied selection of newspapers.

Data availability was a major issue especially with newspapers from non-OECD countries. For example, it was not possible to include any African newspapers except from South Africa. In some cases such as Russia, Japan, China (Hong Kong) or South Africa, the analysis was restricted to national newspapers that are published in the English language. Although the scope and content of these newspapers is likely to be affected by the choice of language, we decided to include these publications in our sample for two reasons: (1) in case of deviations from the 'global mainstream', these newspapers are still likely to reflect these national divergences; and (2) it could also be argued that, in some of these countries such as Russia or China, the fact that these newspapers are published in English allows these publications to remain more independent in terms of freedom of the press, therefore reflecting public opinion in these countries to a higher degree.

Text mining and transformation

For the collection of data, we used databases such as LexisNexis and performed a series of keyword searches. For the search terms, we compiled clusters of key terms related to the concepts included in the analysis. For the terms 'sustainability', 'sustainable development' and 'business ethics', stemming algorithms were developed for the eight different languages included in the sample (English, French, German, Spanish, Portuguese, Dutch, Danish and Italian). This allowed for the inclusion of possible variations in spelling, conjunction or misspelling of key terms.[2] As explained above, for the other more specific concepts of business responsibility, their English terms were mined. For the transformation of data, binary document frequencies (*df*) were accounted for; that is, every article that contained at least one mention of the respective search term in the full text body was included.

$$f(df) = 1, \text{ for } df > 1$$

Not included were descriptive labels used by the newspapers or database operators ('corporate social responsibility' would be one such example). In those cases in which it was not possible to extract those articles that merely contained these descriptive labels,[3] an approximation based on a combination of search functions offered by the respective database was carried out. The search reports obtained from the keyword search were subsequently processed by a text mining routine constructed on the basis of Microsoft Excel. This text mining routine enabled us to link every article that contained a specific search term with the publication date and publication title.

---

2 Interestingly, the use of stemming algorithms helped to identify a large number of slightly misspelled English-language keywords in non-English newspapers: for example, the term 'corporate social responsibility' regularly appeared as 'corporate social respons*a*bility' or 'corporate social respons-abilite' in French newspapers.

3 This refers to newspaper articles in which the descriptive labels are not capitalised: for example, in the case of the Canadian *Globe and Mail* or a number of South African newspapers.

Data analysis

The results of the mining process were converted into frequency tables. As the base unit of analysis, the monthly average number of hits (i.e. articles containing the search term) per newspaper issue was chosen. This allows for comparison of different newspapers, as it takes into account that some newspapers are released daily, whereas others, for example, are only released on weekdays.

$$\text{hits per issue} = \frac{(\textit{total Nb of monthly hits/Nb of days in month})}{(\textit{issues per week/7})}$$

In a first step, the global results as the average of all newspapers included in the analysis were plotted in the form of aggregated line plots. This allows for the identification of overall trends, the amplitudes of seasonal changes, or specific peaks in coverage that may have been triggered by certain events. Subsequently, the monthly averages of hits per newspaper issue were grouped by regions or countries and again displayed as aggregated line plots. For the regional- and country-level analysis, a simple form of moving average smoothing was carried out using 12-month averages (Box and Jenkins 1976; Velleman and Hoaglin 1981). In the case of peaks and deviations from the overall trend, a screening of the mined articles was carried out in order to identify events that triggered these deviations.

Limitations

Data availability was a major issue in sample selection. There is a bias towards newspapers based in OECD countries (76 out of 115 newspapers) and in particular North American and Western European as well as English-language publications (62/115). However, it should be noted that a substantial number of non-OECD newspapers (39) and publications in eight different languages have been included in the sample. Owing to data availability, in the case of Asian newspapers, only English-language publications were considered. Although this may have altered the results significantly, the knowledge gained from these sources was perceived as sufficient reason to include these publications in the sample.

There were slight issues regarding the accuracy and comparability of search terms: the term 'sustainability' carries a broader meaning than, for example, 'corporate citizenship', which has in turn implications for the total level of word frequencies. However, the longitudinal analysis carried out in this study allows for the identification of long-term trends and regional deviations which are not affected by these characteristics of the search terms used. Furthermore, irregularities in the search reports (such as misspelling of terms or the title of a publication, or changes in date format) led to slight errors in data transformation. An error of 1% was tolerated; larger errors were corrected through reiterative adjustment of the text mining tool.

Another issue was the incremental increase of newspapers included in the analysis as a result of improved data availability in the latter stages of the period under review. For example, the majority of South African newspapers were included in the analysis only from July 2006. However, we decided to include these newspapers from the date they became available in order to increase regional diversity of the sample. Finally, a factor that may have affected the results is syndication. However, it is argued that, owing to the sample size and regional diversity, the impact of syndication remains limited.

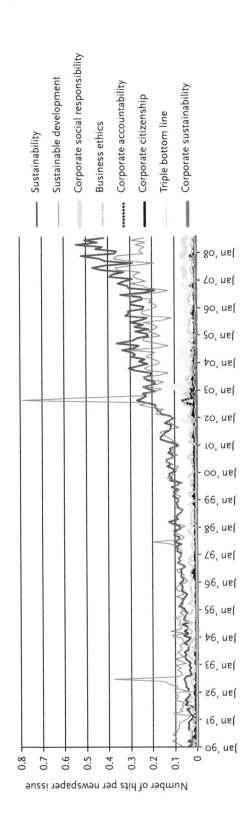

Figure 2 COVERAGE OF VARIOUS (CORPORATE) SUSTAINABILITY-RELATED CONCEPTS

Source: 115 newspapers, January 1990–July 2008

Trends in sustainability

In this section, some key results of the analysis are presented, comprising a longitudinal analysis of: (a) the evolution of core concepts in corporate responsibility and sustainability worldwide; and (b) a comparative analysis of sub-samples of US, UK, South African and South-East Asian newspapers.

Global level

Figure 2 shows the level of coverage of sustainability-related and corporate responsibility-related concepts in 115 leading national newspapers between January 1990 and July 2008.

Overall, a marked increase in the level of coverage of sustainability-related news can be identified. The probability of the terms 'sustainability' or 'sustainable development' appearing in an article of one newspaper issue rose from around 10% in the 1990s to around 30% ('sustainable development') to 50% ('sustainability') towards the end of the period under review. In other words: if today one buys a copy of any leading national newspaper around the globe, the chances of finding the terms 'sustainability' or 'sustainable development' in one language or the other are at least as high as finding a newspaper issue without these terms.

While, until the mid-1990s, 'sustainable development' was clearly the most widespread term, the picture changed in the last decade with 'sustainability' as the less technical term becoming more commonly used. Notable exceptions are the World Summits in Rio de Janeiro 1992, New York 1997 and Johannesburg 2002, triggering clearly identifiable peaks in coverage of sustainable development. However, the coverage remains limited in scope and does not seem to alter the general levels of coverage over a longer period of time before and after these events. Instead, coverage falls back to levels observed two months prior to each event.

Compared with the frequencies of the terms 'sustainability' and 'sustainable development', the other, more business-specific concepts under review remain marginal and mostly appear as background noise, with commonly up to around 0.05 articles per issue. This does not come as a surprise as these concepts are narrower in scope and refer only to corporations as one specific actor in the field of sustainability. However, a closer look at these concepts (Fig. 3) also reveals significant changes in the levels of coverage.

The two concepts with the clearly highest overall number of articles per issue are 'business ethics' and 'corporate social responsibility'. However, the frequency of 'business ethics' seems to decrease slightly within the period under review. In stark contrast, 'corporate social responsibility' can be identified only in the latter half of the review period but experiences the highest increase of all concepts analysed, with frequencies of between 0.04 and 0.06 since 2006. The other four concepts remain marginal throughout the whole period under review, with frequencies commonly well below 0.01. In other words, today about one out of 100 leading national newspapers around the globe contains the term 'corporate citizenship' or 'triple bottom line'. A notable exception is the peak regarding the coverage of both 'corporate accountability' and 'business ethics' in July to September 2002, which is linked to media coverage on US corporate accountability regulation in the aftermath of Enron's 'creative accounting' practices and their consequences. In these three months, both concepts receive coverage of around 0.06 hits per newspaper issue. Another exceptional peak can be identified in autumn 1994 ('business ethics'), linked to increased international coverage of three different accounts of incidents and accusations revolving around corporate malpractice and corruption scandals in the UK, involving Harrods, The Body Shop and high-level UK gov-

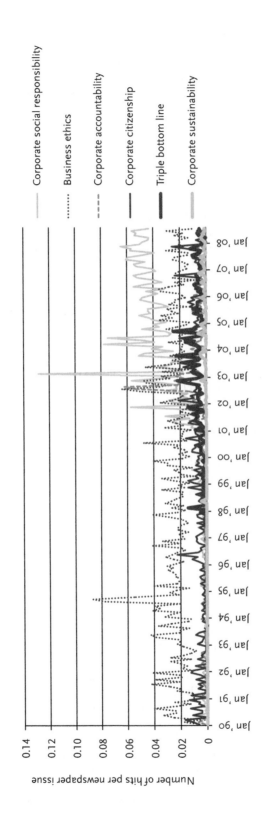

Figure 3 COVERAGE OF VARIOUS CORPORATE RESPONSIBILITY-RELATED CONCEPTS

Source: 115 newspapers, January 1990–July 2008

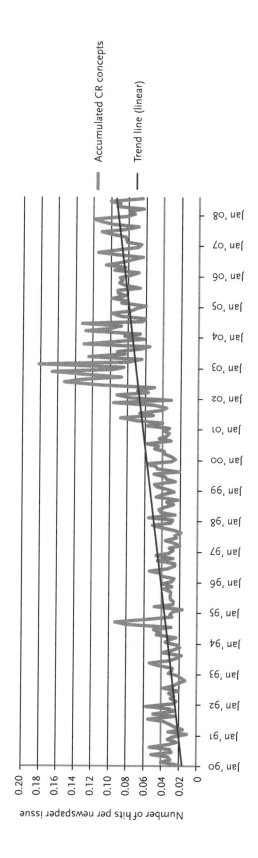

Figure 4 AGGREGATED CONCEPTS OF BUSINESS RESPONSIBILITY (CSR/CORPORATE CITIZENSHIP/CORPORATE ACCOUNTABILITY/CORPORATE SUSTAINABILITY/TBL/BUSINESS ETHICS)

Source: 115 newspapers, January 1990–July 2008

ernment officials. Two peaks in the level of coverage of 'corporate social responsibility' in November 2001 and February 2003 are not linked to particular events, but rather to the publication of special supplements on corporate social responsibility by the UK's *Observer* newspaper.

In summary, it becomes clear that corporate social responsibility has become the most widespread of the concepts referring to the role of business towards society, while the frequency of business ethics has slightly declined. The other concepts, including corporate citizenship, do not seem to have evoked a significant level of usage (and awareness) in the media, and thus remain confined to the academic niche. Figure 4 shows the aggregated frequency of concepts of business responsibility towards society. Despite the downward trend of 'business ethics', the overall coverage on concepts related to the role of business towards society has more than doubled within the period under review, up to an average number of articles per issue of around 0.08. As explained above, the main driver of this development has been the increasingly widespread use of the term 'corporate social responsibility'.

Regional and country level

As described above, overall coverage of both sustainability- and corporate responsibility-related terms has risen significantly since 1990. In this section, the analysis moved to the country level to identify deviations from these 'global' trends. In Figures 5 and 6, data is displayed as 12-month average of hits per newspaper issue. This moving average smoothing facilitates the identification of general trends at the expense of detail. Figure 5 illustrates the development of cumulated frequencies of 'sustainable development' and 'sustainability' for Spain (7 newspapers), France (8), South Africa (8), Australia (7), Germany (7), UK (9), United States (7) as well as eight South-East Asian newspapers (*South China Morning Post* [Hong Kong/China], *Korea Times*, *Korea Herald*, *New Straits Times* [Malaysia], *Manila Times* [Philippines], *The Business Times Singapore*, *The Straits Times* [Singapore] and *The Nation* [Thailand]).

As the regional analysis shows, the development of frequencies is highly unequal. In all eight sub-samples an overall increase from a level of well below 0.25 in the early 1990s can be identified. However, compared with the other sub-samples, the coverage of US newspapers remains fairly constant throughout the period under review, whereas at the other end of the continuum, coverage of Spanish newspapers increases at a pace that resembles exponential growth, up to a level of 2.4 in the first half of 2008. A similar increase can be identified in Australia and France. Unsurprisingly, a peak in the South African newspapers can be observed in the aftermath of the Johannesburg World Summit. A continuous increase, but at a slower pace, can also be identified in German, UK and South-East Asian newspapers. Within the latter sub-sample, a particularly strong increase was observed in the Hong Kong-based *South China Morning Post* and the Malaysian *New Straits Times*.

A likewise heterogeneous development can be identified in a regional- and country-level analysis of the development of different concepts of business responsibility towards society. One of the most striking features of the four graphs in Figure 6 is that, while the level of coverage of corporate social responsibility has increased at an unprecedented pace in recent years in the UK, South Africa and South-East Asia (as it has in the overwhelming majority of all other newspapers included in the analysis), its coverage in the seven US newspapers has remained constant throughout the whole period under review. Here, despite a slight increase in recent years, frequencies of commonly below 0.01 can be observed, whereas in the other three sub-samples, peaks of well above 0.1 can be identified. In the United States, again unlike in the other sub-samples, coverage of corporate social responsibility remains below the level of corporate citizenship, corporate

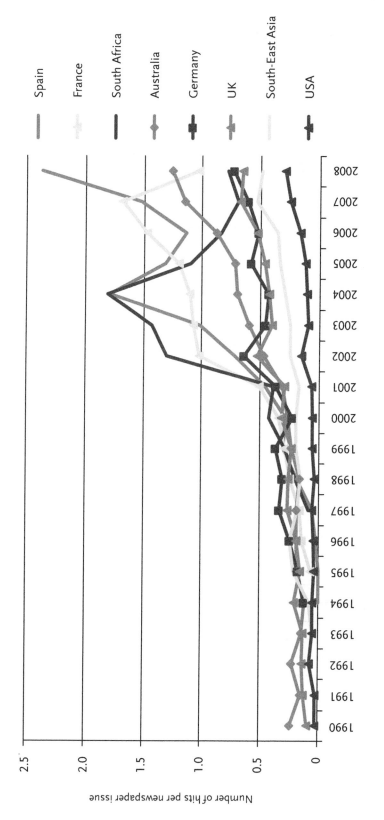

Figure 5 COMBINED FREQUENCY OF THE TERMS 'SUSTAINABLE DEVELOPMENT' AND 'SUSTAINABILITY'; VARIOUS COUNTRY SUB-SAMPLES, JANUARY 1990–JULY 2008

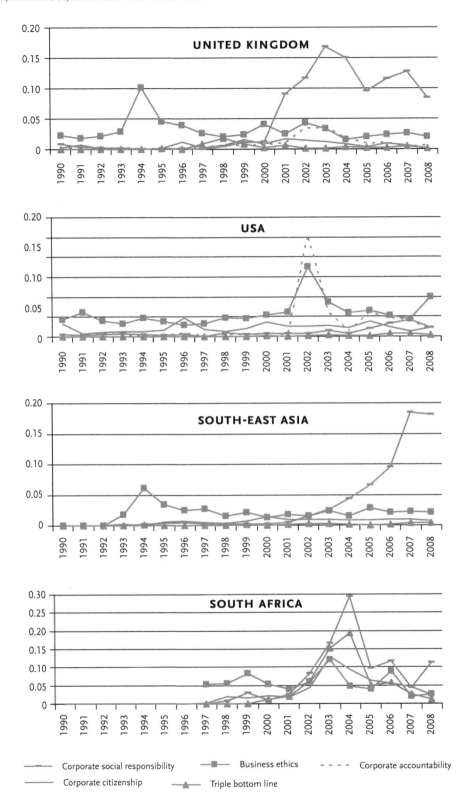

Figure 6 FREQUENCIES OF VARIOUS CONCEPTS OF BUSINESS RESPONSIBILITY TOWARDS SOCIETY IN UK, US, SOUTH-EAST ASIAN AND SOUTH AFRICAN NEWSPAPERS (JANUARY 1990–JULY 2008)

accountability and business ethics, the latter being the most widespread concept. However, with the exception of the Enron scandal and subsequent media coverage in 2002 and 2003, the overall level of coverage of all concepts in US newspapers stays well behind respective levels observed in other countries.

Another interesting feature is that the respective peaks in coverage in the four sub-samples are not only linked to different terminologies, but also occur at different points in time. In the United Kingdom, peaks are reached in 1994 (business ethics) and 2003 (corporate social responsibility); in the United States, one peak can be observed in 2002 (business ethics and corporate accountability); in South-East Asia, a clear peak can be identified in the first half of 2008 (corporate social responsibility); and media coverage in South Africa reaches a peak in 2004 (corporate social responsibility and triple bottom line). South Africa is also the only one of the four sub-samples in which the term 'triple bottom line' seems to be fairly widespread, with frequencies of up to 0.2, whereas in the other three sub-samples it constantly remains below 0.01. Similarly, corporate citizenship reaches a peak average number of articles per issue of 0.12 in South Africa in 2003; in the other three sub-samples, it reaches only levels of up to around 0.01.

Discussion and conclusion

The above longitudinal analysis of global and regional levels of media coverage of concepts related to the role of business towards society proves to be a fruitful area of enquiry. To unfold momentum, current conceptions of corporate responsibility will have to move beyond the academic niche and reach broader public awareness. Especially in the context of current 'mega trends' such as globalisation, global governance and the increasing privatisation of government functions, it can be argued that the broader public ought to play a pivotal role in current conciliatory, 'beyond compliance' wave of business responsibility towards society. Without public awareness and participation, these concepts can be expected to remain somewhat artificial. Therefore, analogously to the veritable explosion of academic work on corporate citizenship and the like in recent years, a more widespread use of all of the concepts under review would have been expected. A number of important points can be derived from the above analysis:

▶ At a global level, an unprecedented increase in the use of both 'sustainability'/'sustainable development' and concepts of business responsibility towards society can be identified in the period under review

▶ Clear regional differences in the coverage of all concepts can be identified

▶ Among the more specific concepts of business responsibility towards society, CSR may have 'taken off', while the overall number of articles per issue of all other concepts remains marginal

▶ Only very few 'global' events can be identified that triggered distinctly higher levels of newspaper coverage in terms of the concepts under review

Increase in use of terms and concepts of business sustainability
On average, aggregated frequencies of 'sustainability' and 'sustainable development' have risen from around 0.1 in the early 1990s up to levels of around 0.5 in recent years. While 'sustainable development' was the dominant term in the first half of the period under review, in the last decade it has been surpassed by 'sustainability' which is now the more widespread term globally. The overall increase does not seem to be related to specific 'global' events. Instead, the increase can be described as incremental. Excep-

tions are the three World Summits in Rio de Janeiro 1992, New York 1997 and Johannesburg 2002 which formed distinct peaks in coverage. However, coverage almost immediately dropped back to levels that had been observed prior to the Rio and Kyoto Summits. Only the 2002 Johannesburg Summit may possibly have had a lasting impact in terms of media attention.

Regarding the various concepts of business responsibility towards society under review, likewise a clear overall increase in the number of articles per issue—albeit at a lower lever—can be identified. Aggregated coverage has quadrupled from an average of 0.02 in 1990 to roughly 0.08 in 2005 to mid-2008, with a number of peaks in 2002–2004. Yet this increase has not taken place uniformly across the different concepts. Instead, the use of 'corporate social responsibility' has increased significantly, whereas, for example, the overall frequencies of 'business ethics' have remained fairly constant.

Regional differences

The regional-level analysis reveals obvious differences in the development of frequencies among newspapers from different countries and regions. This becomes most apparent in the case of the seven US newspapers that have been included in the analysis: regarding all concepts under analysis with the exception of 'business ethics', clear deviations from the global trends can be observed. In general, the levels of coverage among US newspapers remain significantly lower and do not experience a significant increase within the period under review. One noticeable exception is formed by the Enron scandal and its aftermath, triggering comparatively high levels in the frequencies of both business ethics and corporate accountability. In the analysis of frequencies of 'sustainable development' and 'sustainability', remarkably high levels can be identified in France and Spain, both primarily related to increased coverage of sustainable development. In Spain, an average number of articles per issue of above 2.2 in the first half of 2008 was reached, forming the highest level observed in the sample.

Dominance of CSR

With overall frequencies of up to around 0.06 in recent years, corporate social responsibility has become the dominant concept included in the analysis. It has thus surpassed business ethics which on average—albeit at a lower level—used to be the most widespread term in the 1990s. Furthermore, frequencies of business ethics remained fairly constant throughout the period under consideration, whereas, especially since 2002, corporate social responsibility has attracted unprecedented levels of coverage. Interestingly, the highest levels of coverage can be observed in the South African and South-East Asian sub-samples (South Africa: 0.29 in 2004; South-East Asia: 0.19 in 2007), giving ample evidence for the global dissemination of current conceptions of business responsibility.

Compared with the frequency levels observed for corporate social responsibility, all other concepts under review remain either fairly limited (business ethics, corporate accountability) or virtually absent from the public agenda (corporate citizenship, corporate sustainability, triple bottom line) as measured by the number of articles per issue. For example, contrary to John Elkington's assertion that the triple bottom line 'took off' around the turn of the century (Environics International 2001; Elkington 2006), the data shows that, optimistically speaking, the triple bottom line has not yet attracted broader public awareness.

Global events as triggers for newspaper coverage

Based on the results of the analysis, it seems inadequate to interpret the recent developments in the context of sustainability as global in scope. Rather, significant regional deviations from the 'mainstream' seem to prevail. This becomes particularly apparent in the regional analysis of business-specific concepts: despite a general increase that can be observed in all sub-samples except the United States, different peaks related to different concepts as well as different points in time can be observed. A noticeable exception might be the Johannesburg World Summit which possibly altered media attention and triggered higher levels of coverage. In the case of all other 'landmarks', media response seems to be either confined to specific regions or discussion does not seem to occur in the context of the concepts included in the analysis.

Agenda for future research

The above analysis is part of an ongoing project carried out by Queen's University Management School Belfast and Euromed Marseille School of Management. The following set of preliminary research questions forms a part of the future research agenda in this joint project:

▶ How can the different levels of coverage in different countries be explained?

▶ How are the concepts under review represented in the newspapers under review?

▶ Which issues have driven the observed increase in the frequencies of the terms 'sustainable development', 'sustainability' and 'corporate social responsibility'?

▶ Can we identify regional differences in the media representation of these concepts?

Media attention does not of course equate to advances in sustainability, CSR or any other of the concepts. It is, however, unlikely that without public support reflected in increasing media attention there will be significant advances. Ideally, the project will therefore contribute to the understanding of differences in public support and interpretation of these concepts.

References

Banerjee, S.B., E.S. Iyer and R.K. Kashyap (2003) 'Corporate Environmentalism: Antecedents and Influence of Industry Type', *Journal of Marketing* 67.2: 106-22.

Baron, R.M., and D.A. Kenny (1986) 'The Moderator–Mediator Variable Distinction in Social Psychological Research: Conceptual, Strategic, and Statistical Considerations', *Journal of Personality and Social Psychology* 51.6 (December 1986): 1,173-82.

Bijsmans, P., and C. Altides (2007) ' "Bridging the Gap" between EU Politics and Citizens? The European Commission, National Media and EU Affairs in the Public Sphere', *Journal of European Integration* 29.3: 323-40.

Box, G.E.P., and G.M. Jenkins (1976) *Time Series Analysis: Forecasting and Control* (San Francisco: Holden Day, rev. edn).

Boykoff, M.T. (2007) 'Flogging a Dead Norm? Newspaper Coverage of Anthropogenic Climate Change in the United States and United Kingdom from 2003 to 2006', *Area* 39.2: 470-81.

Brossard, D., J. Shanahan and K. McComas (2004) 'Are Issue-Cycles Culturally Constructed? A Comparison of French and American Coverage of Global Climate Change', *Mass Communication and Society* 7.3: 359-77.

Chudnovsky, D., and A. Lopez (1999) *TNCs and the Diffusion of Environmentally Friendly Technologies to Developing Countries* (occasional papers; Copenhagen: UNCTAD/CBS).

Elkington, J. (2006) 'Governance for Sustainability', *Corporate Governance: An International Review* 14.6: 522-29.

Environics International (2001) *CSR and SD Frameworks. Frequency of Mentions 1997–2001* (Toronto: Environics International).

Fayyad, U., G. Piatetsky-Shapiro and P. Smyth (1996) 'From Data Mining to Knowledge Discovery: An Overview', in U. Fayyad, G. Piatetsky-Shapiro, P. Smyth and R. Uthurusamy (eds.), *Advances in Knowledge Discovery and Data Mining* (Cambridge, MA: MIT Press): 1-36.

Feldman, R., and I. Dagan (1995) 'Knowledge Discovery in Textual Databases (KDT)', paper presented at the *First International Conference on Knowledge Discovery and Data Mining (KDD-95)*, Montreal, Canada, 20–21 August 1995.

—— and J. Sanger (2007) *The Text Mining Handbook* (New York: Cambridge University Press).

Hearst, M.A. (1997) 'Text Data Mining: Issues, Techniques, and the Relationship to Information Access', presentation notes for *UW/MS workshop on data mining*, July 1997; people.ischool.berkeley.edu/~hearst/talks/dm-talk, accessed 20 January 2009.

—— (1999) 'Untangling Text Data Mining', paper presented at the *37th Annual Meeting of the Association for Computational Linguistics*, University of Maryland, College Park, MA, 20–26 June 1999.

Jänicke, M. (1996) 'Erfolgsbedingungen von Umweltpolitik', in M. Jänicke (ed.), *Umweltpolitik der Industrieländer. Entwicklung–Bilanz–Erfolgsbedingungen* (Berlin: Edition Sigma): 9-28.

—— (2002) 'The Political System's Capacity for Environmental Policy: The Framework for Comparison', in H. Weidner and M. Jänicke (eds.), *Capacity Building in National Environmental Policy. A Comparative Study of 17 Countries* (Berlin: Springer): 1-18.

——, K. Kern and H. Jörgens (2000) 'Die Diffusion umweltpolitischer Innovationen', *Zeitschrift für Umweltpolitik (ZfU)* 4: 507-46.

Lent, B., R. Agrawal and R. Srikant (1997) 'Discovering Trends in Text Databases', paper presented at the *3rd International Conference on Knowledge Discovery (KDD)*, Newport Beach, CA, 14–17 August 1997.

Lewis, T.L. (2000) 'Media Representations of "Sustainable Development": Sustaining the Status Quo?', *Science Communication* 21.3: 244-73.

Manning, C.D., and H. Schütze (2002) *Foundations of Statistical Natural Language Processing* (Cambridge, MA: MIT Press).

Norris, P. (2001) *Digital Divide: Civic Engagement, Information Poverty and the Internet Worldwide* (Cambridge, UK: Cambridge University Press).

Tan, A.H. (1999) 'Text Mining: The State of the Art and the Challenges', paper presented at the *Pacific-Asia Conference on Knowledge Discovery and Data Mining PAKDD'99 workshop on Knowledge Discovery from Advanced Databases*, Beijing, China, 26 April 1999.

Tews, K., P.-O. Busch and H. Jörgens (2003) 'The Diffusion of New Environmental Policy Instruments', *European Journal of Political Research* 42.4: 569-600.

Valenti, J.M. (2003) 'Commentary: Media Coverage of the World Summit on Sustainable Development', *Science Communication* 24.3: 380-86.

Velleman, P.W., and D.C. Hoaglin (1981) *Applications, Basics, and Computing of Exploratory Data Analysis* (Boston, MA: Duxbury Press).

Vogel, D. (1993) 'Representing Diffuse Interests in Environmental Policy Making', in R.K. Weaver and B.A. Rockman (eds.), *Do Institutions Matter? Government Capabilities in the United States and Abroad* (Washington, DC: The Brookings Institution).

Weidner, H. (2002) 'Capacity Building for Ecological Modernization: Lessons from Cross-national Research', *American Behavioral Scientist* 45.9: 1,340-68.

—— and M. Jänicke (2002a) *Capacity Building in National Environmental Policy. A Comparative Study of 17 Countries* (Berlin: Springer).

—— and M. Jänicke (2002b) 'Summary: Environmental Capacity Building in a Converging World', in H. Weidner and M. Jänicke (eds.), *Capacity Building in National Environmental Policy. A Comparative Study of 17 Countries* (Berlin: Springer): 409-44.

Zyglidopoulos, S.C. (2002) 'The Social and Environmental Responsibilities of Multinationals: Evidence from the Brent Spar Case', *Journal of Business Ethics* 36: 141-51.

Moving the Capital Markets
The EU Emissions Trading Scheme

Rory Sullivan
Insight Investment, UK

Stephanie Pfeifer
Institutional Investors Group on Climate Change, UK

Large institutional investors have significant influence and leverage in society and on the economy. As a consequence, the views that investors hold about issues such as climate change are of critical importance to the manner in which companies respond to these issues.

European institutional investors have recently started to pay much greater attention to climate change; many now analyse climate change-related risks in their investment processes and engage with companies to encourage them to improve their greenhouse gas emissions. In this article we argue that the EU Emissions Trading Scheme (ETS) has been the key catalyst for the growth in European investor interest in climate change, and that the EU ETS should therefore be seen as one of the critical landmarks in the history of corporate responsibility.

We also argue that the broadly positive experience with the EU ETS has contributed to a willingness by investors to engage in the public policy debate around climate change. Investors have been at the forefront of calls for robust, long-term policy targets and effective policy instruments to deliver on these targets. This raises the intriguing prospect of a virtuous circle where effective public policy interventions reinforce investor support for policy action which, in turn, catalyses further policy action.

- EU Emissions Trading Scheme
- Institutional investors
- Climate change

Dr **Rory Sullivan** is Head of Responsible Investment at Insight Investment, where he leads research and engagement activities with a particular focus on climate change. He is also a member of the Steering Committee of the Institutional Investors Group on Climate Change (IIGCC) and Chair of the CBI's Carbon Reporting Working Group. Rory has been widely published on climate change, energy policy and investment issues. He is the author/editor of six books on these issues, including *Corporate Responses to Climate Change* (Greenleaf Publishing, 2008).

✉ 33 Old Broad St, London EC2N 1HZ, UK

🖥 rory.sullivan@insightinvestment.com

🌐 www.insightinvestment.com

Stephanie Pfeifer is Programme Director for the Institutional Investors Group on Climate Change. Stephanie has eight years' experience in the financial sector, having worked as an economist with NatWest, Morgan Grenfell and Deutsche Bank. Stephanie holds an MA in Environmental Change and Management from Oxford University, an MA in European Economics from Exeter University and a BA in Philosophy, Politics and Economics from Oxford University.

✉ Institutional Investors Group on Climate, c/o The Climate Group, The Tower Building, 3rd Floor, York Road, London SE1 7NX, UK

🖥 SPfeifer@theclimategroup.org

🌐 www.iigcc.org

T HE PRIMA FACIE CASE FOR INVESTORS TO BE CONCERNED ABOUT CLIMATE change is clear. Companies may be affected by the weather-related impacts of climate change (e.g. droughts, floods, storms, rising sea levels), public policy measures directed at reducing greenhouse gas emissions and consumer or other pressures to take action on climate change. There may also be opportunities for companies to improve their brand or reputation by taking a proactive approach to responding to climate change or by developing new products or technologies in areas such as renewable energy. The manner in which companies respond to these risks and opportunities may have significant financial implications and may therefore affect the performance of investment portfolios.

In their roles as the proxy owners of companies, as the providers of capital and as wider influences on the structure of society and the economy as a whole, large institutional investors (pension funds, asset managers, insurance companies) have significant influence and leverage. As a consequence, the views that investors hold about issues such as climate change are of critical importance to the manner in which companies respond to these issues (see, generally, Sullivan and Mackenzie 2006a; Sparkes 2002; Tang 2005). Over the past five years, institutional investors have started to pay much greater attention to climate change; many now analyse climate change-related risks in their investment processes, engage with companies to encourage them to improve their greenhouse gas emissions and, albeit to a lesser extent, contribute to public policy discussions on climate change.

In this article we have two objectives. The first, reflecting the focus of this special edition of the *Journal of Corporate Citizenship*, is to set out our view that the EU Emissions Trading Scheme (ETS) has been the key catalyst for the growth in European investor interest in climate change, and that the EU ETS should therefore be seen as one of the critical landmarks in the history of corporate responsibility.[1] The second is to describe and assess the potential implications of investor engagement with public policy. As practitioners in the investment community, we have been struck by the increased willingness of investors to engage in a progressive manner in the public policy debate around climate change. In the latter sections of this article we discuss the potential for this engagement to contribute to the strengthening of climate change policy at the national and international levels.

The current state of play

Investor action on climate change can be broken into three broad areas: investment research and decision-making, company engagement (or activism) and collaboration (including public policy engagement).

---

1 Our view is based on our experience as practitioners and as researchers. We are both involved (Pfeifer as the Programme Director and Sullivan as a member of the steering committee) with the most important European collaborative investor initiative on climate change, the Institutional Investors Group on Climate Change (see www.iigcc.org, accessed 20 January 2009). Furthermore, Sullivan's employer, Insight Investment, is recognised as one of the leading investment managers on climate change, having published a series of major reports on the investment implications of climate change (e.g. Sullivan and Blyth 2006; Sullivan and Kozak 2006; Sullivan 2008a) as well as conducting extensive engagement and research programmes on climate change (see www.insightinvestment.com, accessed 13 January 2009). Finally, we have previously collaborated on research into the motivations for UK institutional investors to pay greater attention to climate change in their investment processes (Pfeifer 2005; Pfeifer and Sullivan 2008).

Investment research

Before discussing the current state of play on investment research and investment decision-making, it is important to first explain why this is important to corporate behaviour.[2] The basic argument is that, collectively, the financial analysis and investment decision-making of stock market participants sets the share price for companies. Share prices, in turn, affect company behaviour, both directly by affecting the cost of capital, and indirectly by motivating boards and executive behaviour. If investment analysis fails to place sufficient weight on the value of good corporate social and environmental performance or on the costs of poor performance, then the capital markets may create incentives for companies to cause (or fail to prevent) harmful corporate impacts on society and the environment.

The volume of research published on the investment implications of climate change has grown significantly since the first substantive broker (or sell-side) research reports on climate change were produced in 2003. Most of this research has focused on the financial implications of the EU ETS, in particular for the electricity sector (Hagart and Knoepfel 2008; Pfeifer and Sullivan 2008). The EU ETS was critical to this upsurge in the volume of investment research as it gave greenhouse gas emissions, at least from the European industrial facilities covered by the scheme, a financial value, and so made these emissions a factor that needed to be (and could be) considered in investment analysis. Other research that has been published includes reports on the investment implications of other European climate change policy initiatives (e.g. aviation and emissions trading, proposals to regulate CO_2 emissions from automobiles), country-specific policies on wind and renewable energy, and potential emissions trading or other policy measures in countries outside the EU.

However, far less attention—with the notable exception of the insurance and reinsurance sectors—has been paid to the physical impacts of climate change (Hagart and Knoepfel 2008). While a number of broker reports have examined issues such as drought in Australia and specific types of extreme weather event, these reports remain few in number and pay relatively little attention to the specific causes of these events or the likelihood of such events being repeated in the future.

This picture is reflected in the manner in which investment managers are looking at climate change. Even though investment managers report that they are increasing the attention they pay to climate change and are building their capacity to analyse the financial implications of new regulations, the main areas of focus are those areas where there are clear investment opportunities (in particular, sectors such as renewable energy that have received significant government support and/or are beneficiaries of high oil and coal prices) and those sectors—electricity utilities, cement and other heavy industries—that are directly exposed to climate change regulation (see, for example, the survey results in IIGCC 2008 and Carbon Trust 2008).

Despite this progress, substantial barriers still remain to the further integration of climate change into investment analysis. First, many of the impacts of climate change are predicted to occur over much longer time-frames than those typically used by investors; the short-term nature of investment mandates means that investment managers tend to focus on short-term drivers of investment performance rather than longer-term risks and opportunities. Second, policy uncertainty—including the degree of government support for international policy action on climate change, the specific targets and policy instruments that will be adopted at the international and national levels, and the relationship between climate policy goals and other policy goals such as energy security and diversity of supply (see, further, Sullivan and Blyth 2006)—remains

---

2 For a more extensive treatment of this argument, see Mackenzie 2006.

a significant issue. Third, the assessment of climate change-related risks and opportunities is compounded by the general inadequacy of corporate disclosures in this area (Sullivan and Kozak 2006; Sullivan 2008a).

Engagement/activism

Investors are a key influence on company decision-making and actions and the views that investors hold on issues such as climate change are therefore an important, although not necessarily the most important, determinant of how companies will behave (Hoffman 2006: 54; Sullivan and Mackenzie 2008). An increasing number of institutional investors (see the data presented in IIGCC 2008) are engaging with companies on climate change and related issues. The objectives of most of this engagement have been to improve corporate climate change reporting and to encourage companies to integrate climate change into their business strategies and risk management systems. However, many issues, including adaptation to unavoidable climate change[3] and climate-friendly product design, presently receive relatively limited attention. Furthermore, mainstream investors have shown limited appetite for asking companies to reduce greenhouse gas emissions beyond those that would be justified in financial terms (see, for example, Carbon Trust 2008: 11).

The drivers for investors to engage with companies have been quite different from those for investment research. In interviews with investment managers and pension funds, a range of contributory factors were highlighted (Pfeifer 2005; Pfeifer and Sullivan 2008). These included the strengthening of the scientific evidence regarding climate change (in particular the work of the Intergovernmental Panel on Climate Change [IPCC]),[4] the publication of the *Stern Review on the Economics of Climate Change* (Stern 2006), the release of Al Gore's film *An Inconvenient Truth*, the leadership role of certain pension funds (in particular the Universities Superannuation Scheme and its 2001 report analysing the investment implications of climate change [Mansley and Dlugolecki 2001]) and asset managers (e.g. Insight, F&C, CIS), and the introduction of the EU ETS and other policy measures in areas such as renewable energy. What has been interesting is that the tone of investor engagement has progressively strengthened and the number of investors engaging with companies has increased (see, for example, IIGCC 2008). There have been two important reasons for this (Pfeifer 2005). The first is that the nature of the press coverage has changed dramatically. Specifically, the volume of coverage has increased, the tone has changed from scepticism regarding the science of climate change to broad acceptance of the scientific predictions, the focus has moved from the science to the policy and other actions required, the issue has moved from the science and environmental pages to the business pages and, perhaps most significantly, climate change is now routinely covered in business publications such as the *Financial Times*). The second has been the EU ETS, which has, as discussed further below, sent a clear signal to investors that governments can and will act to regulate greenhouse gas emissions and, therefore, that it is in investors' interest to encourage companies to take action to better manage their emissions.

---

3 Four major UK institutional investors—two asset managers (Insight Investment and Henderson Global Investors) and two pension funds (USS and Railpen)—initiated a collaborative research project on adaptation in mid-2007. The project will identify the major adaptation-related risks for a number of sectors. It is expected that investors will use this information as the starting point for investment research on this issue and as the basis for their dialogue with companies and policy-makers (see, further, Sullivan *et al.* 2008).

4 www.ipcc.ch, accessed 13 January 2009.

Collaboration

The number of investors participating in collaborative initiatives on climate change has also grown; the drivers for investors to participate in these initiatives are broadly similar to those for engagement discussed above (Pfeifer 2005; Pfeifer and Sullivan 2008). The most important of these collaborative initiatives are the (European) Institutional Investors Group on Climate Change (IIGCC)[5] whose objectives are to engage with companies on their climate strategies and to emphasise to policy-makers the need for long-term policy targets in order to provide an environment facilitating long-term investment decision-making (Sullivan *et al.* 2005) and the Carbon Disclosure Project (CDP)[6] which solicits, on behalf of institutional investors, climate change-related information from some of the world's largest listed companies.

While CDP's focus on improving corporate disclosure is relatively uncontroversial (as it fits comfortably within the scope of what investors see as their self-interest), the IIGCC's work, in particular its public policy engagement, represents a major extension of investors' work on climate change. IIGCC's public policy work is aimed at encouraging public policy-makers to take account of the long-term interests of institutional investors. Since 2005, IIGCC has made a series of submissions to government inquiries and consultations relating to issues such as Phase II of the EU ETS, the inclusion of aviation in the EU ETS, and EU Action on Climate Change post-2012.[7] In these submissions, IIGCC emphasised the importance of policy certainty, the need for long-term policy targets directed at significant reductions in greenhouse gas emissions, the desirability of extending the use of economic instruments and incentives, and the need for better corporate disclosures.

In the context of this discussion about the role of the EU ETS, what has been interesting has been that the IIGCC has maintained—and even strengthened—its messages since 2005 (i.e. since the introduction of the EU ETS). Anecdotally, from our discussions with asset manager and asset owner representatives, investors have become more comfortable with the argument that well-designed policy on climate change should provide significant financial benefits and/or have minimal impact on overall investment performance, and that they should therefore seek to influence the policy process. There also seems to be an acceptance that governments, at least within Europe, are intent on taking substantive action on climate change and so there is limited value to be gained from taking an oppositional position on policy in this area.

A wider perspective on the EU emissions trading scheme

The central role that has been played by the ETS in finance and climate change policy debates has received relatively little attention in the climate change literature. This is probably unsurprising given the controversies that bedevilled the ETS in its first phase of operation (2005–2007): some EU Member States over-allocated emission permits (leading to permit prices falling to virtually zero having risen to almost €30 per tonne of CO_2 at one point); there were concerns about the manner in which permits were allocated (most were allocated for free rather than through auctioning, and allocations were

---

5 www.iigcc.org (accessed 13 January 2009). Similar organisations exist in North America (the International Network on Climate Risk, INCR) and Australia and New Zealand (the Investor Group on Climate Change, IGCC).

6 www.cdproject.net (accessed 13 January 2009).

7 See the IIGCC website for a comprehensive listing: www.iigcc.org/activities/activity4.aspx (accessed 13 January 2009).

based on historic emissions); and significant benefits (windfall profits) accrued to European electricity generation companies.

These controversies have obscured the critical contributions that the ETS has made since it was introduced. Perhaps most importantly, it has moved climate change from the private (or voluntary) to the public space (see, for example, Pinske and Kolk 2007).[8] As a mandatory requirement, it has established a price for greenhouse gas emissions (with price reflected in electricity power prices), has enabled the development of robust institutional structures to support emissions trading, has led to the development of a huge emissions trading market, and has resulted in a significant level of learning among all relevant players (including governments and companies) about the practicalities of operating (and operating in) a full-scale emissions trading market. While these are all important and necessary building blocks for any future strengthening of emissions trading as a climate change policy instrument, whether within the EU or elsewhere, it is probably too early to draw firm conclusions on the impact of EU ETS on greenhouse gas emissions. In the electricity sector (where the strongest emission reduction targets have been imposed), emissions trading has influenced the dispatch decision (i.e. whether to generate electricity using coal or gas). However, as yet, there is limited evidence that emissions trading has led to significant investment in cleaner (or lower-emitting) forms of power generation. Even though there have been a number of pilot and research and development projects on clean coal combustion and carbon capture and storage, we have yet to see firm proposals for the deployment of these technologies at scales comparable to conventional power stations. Because of uncertainties around the post-2012 international regime and the specific targets that the electricity sector will be required to meet, most of the generating companies are adopting a wait-and-see approach and minimising capital expenditures on new power stations until the future direction of policy is clearer (see, generally, Sullivan and Blyth 2006).

It is pertinent to note that electricity companies have made quite significant investments in renewable energy, most notably wind. While renewable forms of power generation are obvious beneficiaries of an emissions trading scheme, the primary motivation for these types of investment does not appear to have been the EU ETS. Rather, in those countries that have seen significant increases in these investments, the primary reason has been the direct financial support (whether through subsidies, specific feed-in tariffs or other forms of fiscal support) that makes these technologies cost-competitive with conventional fossil fuels. From discussions with electricity companies, the key feature of these policy regimes has been their dependability; governments are seen as being strongly committed to supporting these policy measures over time and 'stroke of the pen' risk (where government dramatically changes its policy approach) is seen as much lower.

Looking beyond the electricity sector, the evidence is that EU ETS has contributed to companies increasing the importance they assign to climate change as a business issue (see generally the case studies and analysis in Sullivan 2008b), although analysis of the manner in which companies view climate change-related risks and opportunities suggests that climate change is seen as either a compliance requirement (see for example Pinske and Kolk 2007) or as an efficiency measure (see Sullivan 2008a) but not as a key strategic business issue. It is interesting to note that corporate rhetoric on climate change as a business issue seems divergent from business practice. For example, a recent McKinsey (*McKinsey Quarterly* 2007) survey suggested that 60% of global executives view climate change as important to consider within their companies' overall

---

8 More generally, the UK Carbon Trust has argued that 'Regulation is usually the key initiator of change although the cost of carbon is not the decisive factor in many sectors' (Carbon Trust 2008: 3). See also PricewaterhouseCoopers 2008: iv.

strategy and nearly 70% see it as an important consideration for managing corporate reputation and brand. However, relatively few companies seem to be translating this rhetoric into tangible action, with 44% of CEOs noting that climate change is not a significant item on their agendas and many respondents reporting that climate change is considered only occasionally when managing corporate reputation and brands or developing new products.

The effects of the EU ETS have been wider than the simple integration of climate change-related risks and opportunities into mainstream investment decision-making in those sectors where greenhouse gas emissions present a financially material risk (or opportunity). It is our view that the EU ETS has catalysed a more fundamental change; investors are taking the threat of climate change regulation in countries/regions where there is presently no such regulation extremely seriously. The fact that emissions trading has been successfully established and retained political support has not only encouraged similar initiatives elsewhere in the world (e.g. the voluntary trading schemes in the United States and the proposed Australian/New Zealand emissions trading scheme) but has also signalled to companies and investors that policy-makers can and will act on climate change. Demonstrating that further regulation is seen as a credible possibility, over the period 2006–2008, a number of broker research reports were published focusing on impending or proposed climate change regulations in countries such as Australia, the United States, Canada and Japan.[9]

Finally, the EU ETS has been the most visible example of policy-makers' willingness to act on climate change. The fact that the EU has introduced the scheme and has maintained it even when permit prices rose to €30/tonne suggests that, at least at this level, the economic consequences of emissions trading can be accepted by European policy-makers. That is, despite the uncertainties about the exact details of climate change policy beyond 2012, there is a general recognition that there will be some form of emissions trading and that political support for emissions trading will remain at least up to this level of carbon price. The political support for the EU ETS has had a profound impact on the dialogue that investors have with companies. Anecdotally, investors' discussions with companies have moved from whether there will be a carbon price (or some sort of regulatory mechanism) for greenhouse gas emissions to the starting premise that there will be some form of cost associated with these emissions; discussion then focuses on how companies are positioning themselves to respond to these costs over the short and long term.

Discussion: investors and public policy

The final issue we would like to explore in this article is 'where to from here?' While we have highlighted the critical role that has been played by the EU ETS in catalysing investor interest in climate change, we are also very aware that investor action on climate change (in terms of investment analysis and engagement) can be seen as falling within fairly constrained parameters. More specifically, investor engagement can be described as encouraging companies to take action to reduce their emissions to the extent justified by current and plausible future regulatory scenarios, with the assumptions underpinning this engagement including the expectation that governments will protect or at least

---

9 The investor interest in impending climate change legislation mirrors the manner in which companies are proactively engaging with voluntary greenhouse gas emissions trading schemes in countries outside the European Union (see, for example, the case studies in Sullivan 2008b). The literature suggests that some firms (albeit a minority) are anticipating and preparing for the introduction of mandatory emissions trading schemes (Hoffman 2006: 47; Pinske and Kolk 2007).

minimise the impact on existing industry players and that companies will have time to react when necessary (see, for example, Carbon Trust 2008: 4). This engagement can be seen as consistent with but not extending beyond the boundaries that would be set by a conventional cost–benefit analysis; certainly this direct engagement is not, in the main, pushing companies to take action that would be damaging to their short-term commercial interests. Given that pension funds operate under trust law, which imposes a 'fiduciary' obligation on the trustees and fund managers involved to serve the interests (usually interpreted in exclusively financial terms) of those whose money is invested in these funds, it is not clear that it is reasonable or legally permissible to expect pension funds to go beyond this point (Sullivan and Mackenzie 2006b; for a challenge to this view see Freshfields Bruckhaus Deringer 2005).

Having noted this limitation, we have been struck by the willingness of institutional investors over the past few years—perhaps emboldened by the experience of the EU ETS—to play a constructive role in public policy debates around climate change. Investors have been at the forefront of calls for robust, long-term policy targets and effective policy instruments to deliver on these targets, in particular through the IIGCC. This raises the intriguing prospect of a virtuous circle where effective public policy interventions reinforce investor support for policy action which, in turn, catalyses further policy action. As we have seen with the EU ETS, public policy is critical, not only because of its direct effect and influence on corporate behaviour but because of its ability to reinforce the effectiveness of investor engagement, providing support to investors' arguments that companies need to prepare themselves for further policy action over time.

The question is whether this type of engagement runs counter to investors' fiduciary duty obligations. Our view is that the answer is probably no, as we believe that well-designed public policy should provide very significant benefits to institutional investors. There are a number of different strands to this argument (for a more detailed account of this argument see Sullivan and Mackenzie 2008). First, on a macroeconomic basis, the short-term costs should be outweighed by the longer-term economic benefits. For example, the International Energy Agency (IEA 2006) argues that countries could implement a range of measures directed at reducing energy demand growth and greenhouse gas emissions and increasing energy security, where the benefits of using and producing energy more efficiently significantly outweigh the costs incurred. Second, the actions that may be in the interest of an individual company—in this particular case, allowing increasing greenhouse gas emissions—may not be in the long-term interests of the economy as a whole as such emissions may expose other companies to the physical impacts of climate change.[10] Third, well-designed public policy should provide significant opportunities for companies. Benefits should be realised through, for example, identifying new technologies, capturing new markets or reducing the need for defensive expenditures (e.g. to respond to increased risks of floods or extreme weather events).

Conclusions

We believe that the EU ETS has been the critical influence on investors' views on climate change over the past few years. Climate change has moved from a niche 'SRI' (socially responsible investment) issue to a mainstream investment issue, to the point where investors expect there to be a long-term price of carbon in many major markets and expect the pressure on companies to reduce their emissions to increase. Furthermore,

---

10 There is a growing literature on the idea of institutional investors as 'universal owners' (see further Hawley and Williams 2000).

the outcomes from the ETS—in particular the fact that some of the more catastrophic predictions around economic collapse have not resulted!—have encouraged investors to engage with public policy on climate change with at least some confidence that a properly designed, long-term policy framework will not be damaging to investment (or to investors' interests) and may in fact provide real benefits to investors.

We do not want to overstate the role or contribution of investors, as we recognise that investors are just one of the influences on corporate behaviour, that the outcomes from investor engagement will, inevitably, be limited by the manner in which companies define their self-interest, and that enhanced analysis is, at best, a very blunt instrument for influencing corporate behaviour. However, the growing willingness of investors to engage with policy-makers in an effort to change the 'rules of the game', in our view, means that government can look to investors as an ally, rather than an opponent, in taking the radical policy actions that are essential if we are to respond effectively to the threat to our planet presented by climate change. For that fact alone, the EU ETS should be seen as one of the key landmarks in the history of corporate responsibility.

References

Carbon Trust (2008) *Climate Change: A Business Revolution?* (London: Carbon Trust).

Freshfields Bruckhaus Deringer (2005) *A Legal Framework for the Integration of Environmental, Social and Governance Issues into Institutional Investment* (Geneva: United Nations Environment Programme Finance Initiative).

Hagart, G., and I. Knoepfel (2008) *Research Centre Stage: Four Years of the Enhanced Analytics Initiative* (Zurich: onValues).

Hawley, J., and A. Williams (2000) *The Rise of Fiduciary Capitalism* (Philadelphia, PA: University of Pennsylvania Press).

Hoffman, A. (2006) *Getting Ahead of the Curve: Corporate Strategies that Address Climate Change* (Arlington, VA: Pew Center on Global Climate Change).

IEA (International Energy Agency) (2006) *World Energy Outlook 2006* (Paris: IEA).

IIGCC (Institutional Investors Group on Climate Change) (2008) *Investor Statement Report 2007* (London: IIGCC).

Mackenzie, C. (2006) 'The Scope for Investor Action on Corporate Social and Environmental Impacts', in R. Sullivan and C. Mackenzie (eds.), *Responsible Investment* (Sheffield, UK: Greenleaf Publishing): 20-38.

Mansley, M., and A. Dlugolecki (2001) *Climate Change: A Risk Management Challenge for Institutional Investors* (London: Universities Superannuation Scheme [USS]).

The McKinsey Quarterly (2007) 'How Companies Think about Climate Change: A McKinsey Global Survey', *The McKinsey Quarterly*, December 2007.

Pfeifer, S. (2005) *Institutional Investors and Climate Change: An Analysis of the Integration of Climate Change Risks and Opportunities into Investment Decision-making* (MSc dissertation; Oxford, UK: University of Oxford).

—— and R. Sullivan (2008) 'Public Policy, Institutional Investors and Climate Change: A UK Case Study', *Climatic Change* 89: 245-62.

Pinske, J., and A. Kolk (2007) 'Multinational Corporations and Emissions Trading: Strategic Responses to New Institutional Constraints', *European Management Journal* 25.6: 441-52.

PricewaterhouseCoopers (2008) *Carbon Disclosure Project 2008: Global 500* (London: Carbon Disclosure Project).

Sparkes, R. (2002) *Socially Responsible investment: A Global Revolution* (Chichester, UK: John Wiley).

Stern, N. (2006) *Stern Review: The Economics of Climate Change* (Cambridge, UK: Cambridge University Press).

Sullivan, R. (2008a) *Taking the Temperature: Assessing the Performance of Large UK and European Companies in Responding to Climate Change* (London: Insight Investment).

—— (ed.) (2008b) *Corporate Responses to Climate Change: Achieving Emissions Reductions through Regulation, Self-regulation and Economic Incentives* (Sheffield, UK: Greenleaf Publishing).

—— and W. Blyth (2006) *Climate Change Policy Uncertainty and the Electricity Industry: Implications and Unintended Consequences* (Chatham House Briefing Paper EEDP BP 06/02; London: Chatham House).

—— and J. Kozak (2006) *The Climate Change Disclosures of European Electricity Utilities* (London: Insight Investment).

—— and C. Mackenzie (eds.) (2006a) *Responsible Investment* (Sheffield, UK: Greenleaf Publishing).

—— and C. Mackenzie (2006b) 'Introduction', in R. Sullivan and C. Mackenzie (eds.), *Responsible Investment* (Sheffield, UK: Greenleaf Publishing): 12-19.

—— and C. Mackenzie (2008) 'Can Investor Activism Play a Meaningful Role in Addressing Market Failures?', *Journal of Corporate Citizenship* 31: 77-88.

——, N. Robins, D. Russell and H. Barnes (2005) 'Investor Collaboration on Climate Change: The Work of the IIGCC', in K. Tang (ed.), *The Finance of Climate Change* (London: Risk Books): 197-210.

——, D. Russell and N. Robins (2008) 'Managing the Unavoidable: Understanding the Investment Implications of Adapting to Climate Change' (London: Insight Investment/Henderson Global Investors/USS/Railpen).

Tang, K. (ed.) (2005) *The Finance of Climate Change* (London: Risk Books).

Taking Prahalad High-Tech

The Emergence and Evolution of Global Corporate Citizenship in the IT Industry

Anke Schwittay

University of California at Berkeley, USA

In this paper, I analyse the emergence and evolution of e-Inclusion, HP's flagship global corporate citizenship programme, as a landmark in the history of corporate citizenship in the IT industry. This programme, which existed from 2000 to 2005, was the first explicit attempt by a major high-tech company to operationalise the theories of C.K. Prahalad, by implementing a direct and an indirect bottom-of-the-pyramid (bop) strategy. The first led to the development of pilot programmes that worked directly with the rural poor to test bop products, services and business models and to create new sources of income for project participants. The second strategy saw e-Inclusion establish collaborations with public-sector organisations which until then had been peripheral to HP's business, but were recognised as vital for e-Inclusion's operations and HP's emerging market success. I argue that important lessons can be drawn from this flagship corporate citizenship programme, which can make current IT initiatives more sustainable and meaningful.

- IT industry
- Silicon Valley
- Hewlett-Packard
- Digital divide
- Emerging markets
- C.K. Prahalad
- Bottom of the pyramid
- Corporate citizenship
- India
- South Africa

Anke Schwittay is an anthropologist working at the intersection of social innovation, technology and international development. She obtained her PhD from the University of California at Berkeley, where she also teaches. She is the author of *Silicon Valley's Emerging Markets: Global Corporate Citizenship and Entrepreneurship in the IT Industry*. Anke is the Co-founder and Director of Research of the RiOS Institute, as well as an adjunct professor at the Presidio School of Management.

✉ UC Berkeley, Department of Anthropology, 232 Kroeber Hall, Berkeley, CA 94720, USA

🖥 schwitta@berkeley.edu

O N 16 OCTOBER 2000, CARLY FIORINA, CEO OF THE HEWLETT-PACKARD Company (HP), announced the launch of the company's e-Inclusion initiative at the Creating Digital Dividends conference in Seattle.[1] In her keynote address, she argued that companies could not afford to ignore the innovative potential of 4 billion people, nor the growth—in particular in ICT (information and communication technologies) spending—of emerging markets (Fiorina 2000). To tap this potential, HP had:

> developed a major new corporate initiative to reach the emerging market economies— or what we could just as easily call the excluded market economies. And we are focusing it directly on the rural poor in Africa, Asia, Latin America and Central Europe (Fiorina 2000).

The 300 people listening to her speech included corporate, government and civil society leaders, from Bill Gates to Jeff Bezos, founder and CEO of Amazon.com; from Chandrababu Naidu, the Chief Minister of the Indian state of Andhra Pradesh, to Mohsen Khalil, the director of the World Bank's ICT programme; and from Vinton Cerf, the 'father of the Internet', to Iqbal Kadir, the co-founder of Grameenphone. Their gathering took place in Seattle less than a year after the same city had been on fire during the meetings of the World Trade Organisation (WTO), which were derailed by an international coalition of diverse groups—environmental advocates, labour unions, human rights activists and 'anti-globalisation' networks—which protested against the lack of public accountability of multinational corporations and global institutions such as the WTO. What became known as the 'Battle of Seattle' revealed the public wariness of a globalisation driven by corporate and capitalist interests. In response, corporate leaders accelerated their efforts to portray business as a responsible and beneficial force in society and to develop actions and programmes that would give life to this portrayal. The Creating Digital Dividend Conference was the first concerted action of the high-tech industry.

On day two of the conference, C.K. Prahalad presented his ideas about the market opportunities offered by the 4 billion poor of this world. Over the next few years, he popularised these ideas through publications in academic journals, a book and another high-profile conference in San Francisco in December 2004, entitled *Eradicating Poverty through Profit*.[2] Fiorina took centre stage here once again, giving the convening keynote in which she presented e-Inclusion's achievements over the last four years. It was one of her last public appearances, as she was forced to resign two months later. Her successor, Mark Hurd, terminated the programme as part of his cost-cutting measures. In spite of its demise, e-Inclusion, and the IT industry in general, presents a good example to illuminate the brief history of corporate citizenship, for a number of reasons.

First, the increasing centrality of information and communication technologies (ICTs) in our lives has also heightened concerns about the digital divide, which is the gap between those who have access to such technologies and the advantages they offer and those who do not. The high-tech industry has risen to this challenge with what Craig Warren Smith has called 'digital corporate citizenship'; it is these efforts that make the industry a leader in the corporate citizenship area (Smith 2002). And no other IT company has done more to champion the social engagements of the industry than HP: the

---

1 At the time of its launch, the programme was called World e-Inclusion; *world* was dropped from the title in 2001.
2 During that conference, concerns about the bottom-of-the-pyramid (bop) model included: brain and capital drain to the north, transnational corporations' (TNCs') contributions to the growth of strong, local economies and equitable wealth distribution, the creation of an unsustainable consumer culture, the enslavement of the poor to credit and the subsidisation of TNCs to the detriment of local businesses.

company donated its first five dollars to local charities only two years after its founding in 1938; David Packard was laughed at ten years later for telling a gathering of corporate executives that companies had larger civic responsibilities; and HP included 'good citizenship' in its first corporate objectives published in 1957 (Collins and Porras 1994; Packard 1995; Willmott 2001; Malone 2007). This makes the company a good place to study the evolution of corporate citizenship.

e-Inclusion continued that tradition; at the time of its launch *Fortune* magazine called it 'the most visionary step ever taken by an IT company' (quoted in Smith 2002: 5). It also was one of the first programmes that made the strategic nature of corporate citizenship initiatives, which aim to do well by doing good, explicit. And it did so by using the ideas of C.K. Prahalad, who commented that 'because of HP, [the poor] are now a legitimate subject of senior management discussion' (quoted in Kirkpatrick 2001). He was referring to e-Inclusion, and the following case study of the programme will focus on its use of bop theories, the challenges of their implementation, as well as lessons learned.[3] The paper will conclude with an examination of how current digital divide initiatives of IT leaders can benefit from the lessons of this landmark corporate citizenship programme.

Global corporate citizenship at HP

e-Inclusion was HP's flagship global corporate citizenship programme from 2000 to 2005. Its mission, 'to close the gap between the technology empowered and the technology excluded communities on our planet by making it profitable to do so', showed the strategic nature of e-Inclusion, and of corporate citizenship programmes in general. e-Inclusion aimed to achieve its double objective by opening up new markets for the company at the bottom of the pyramid (bop). On the one hand, what I call an indirect bop strategy was focusing greater attention on public-sector institutions, such as multilateral development organisations and developing-country governments, which until then had been peripheral to HP's business. On the other hand, e-Inclusion also developed a direct bop strategy whereby it worked directly with the poor in pilot projects. The aim was to develop and test new bop products, services and business models, while at the same time providing novel sources of income for project participants.

e-Inclusion evolution

The impetus for e-Inclusion came from environmental sustainability efforts at HP in the mid-1990s. Among them were the *Celebration of Creativity* events and the *World's Best Industrial Research Lab* initiative at HP Labs, and the *HP for Sustainability* conference, where Stuart Hart gave a keynote speech about the profitability of green business (Hart 1997). After reading Alex Count's book about Muhammad Yunus and the Grameen Bank, one of e-Inclusion's co-founders began to think about a 'parallel paradigm shift' for HP: turning previously excluded customers into a new market for the company, and replacing philanthropic handouts with help that enables the poor to help themselves (Waugh 2001). She met Yunus when both served on the board of the State of the World Forum that convened in San Francisco in 1997, and Bangladesh was one of World e-Inclusion's first, albeit very short-lived, project sites.

---

3 This case study is based on 12 months of ethnographic fieldwork at HP's headquarters and e-Inclusion implementation sites in 2003. All quotes from HP employees and project participants are based on personal interviews conducted by the authors during that time.

In the spring of 2000, a senior executive who was inspired by Prahalad's theories about eradicating poverty through profit, which were beginning to circulate on the Internet, took his idea of a programme that would harness HP technologies and business expertise towards this end to Fiorina, who by all accounts immediately liked it.[4] HP managers were also enticed by success stories such as that of Hindustan Lever.[5] As one of the first e-Inclusion employees told me, Hindustan Lever served his group as an example, 'although I think what we are doing is more significant than soap'.

Fiorina gave orders to Debra Dunn, Senior VP of Corporate Affairs and Global Citizenship, to put together a group, and in June 2000 the company launched e-Inclusion internally. The initial budget was small; actual figures have never been made public because, according to one co-founder, 'people would have seen that the expenditures were very small compared to the hype and hoopla around the programme'. The budget did allow the co-founders to hire their first employees, and once again they followed Prahalad's advice to bring together a diverse group of people in 'skunk work teams that ignore conventional dogma' (Prahalad and Hammond 2002: 55). Correspondingly, e-Inclusion's first employees were 'out-of-the-box' people who were passionate about changing the world through corporate actions: an organic farmer, a former Peace Corps worker, a self-styled corporate revolutionary.

Because HP wanted to build a new ecosystem around its e-Inclusion work, it recruited James Moore to head the programme's international advisory board, which included academics, human rights activists and entrepreneurs working in emerging markets. e-Inclusion's first business plan identified the rural poor, and rural women in particular, as the most needy groups. As traditional small farmer 'subjects' of development, the former have for several decades been the target of programmes for efficient agricultural commercialisation (Escobar 1995). Development experts have also focused on women as the best way to improve their families' lives, and it was Yunus's microfinance revolution that implemented these ideas on a global scale, with important implications for the social welfare conditions of rural women (Rankin 2001).[6]

In keeping with HP's foray into the Internet at the time, e-Inclusion wanted to enable the rural poor to use the Internet as a tool to generate income, through accessing information and a variety of e-services, from commerce to banking to health and education. The programme's first site was Costa Rica, where e-Inclusion partnered with the Costa Rican Foundation for Sustainable Development, led by former President José María Figueres, on the LINCOS project (Braund and Schwittay 2006).[7] LINCOS turned recycled shipping containers into rural Internet access centres, and HP outfitted the first two containers to the cost of US$115,000, in the hope of generating contracts for hundreds more (HP's Strategic Corporation Agreement of 2000, unpublished).

---

4 Fiorina became HP's CEO in July 1999. As an outsider in more than one sense (a woman from the East Coast among the Silicon Valley high-tech old-boy club and a marketing executive in an engineering company), her choice was surprising. Her attempts to transform HP's paternalistic, laid-back, mild-mannered and consensus-driven culture, known as the HP Way, into an aggressive and hard-charging work style did not enamour her to many HP employees (Anders 2003; Burrows 2003; Caudron 2003). Her most controversial move was the merger with Compaq computers, which pitted the company against the families of David Packard and Bill Hewlett who had founded HP in 1938 in Palo Alto, California.

5 One of the classic success stories of bop approaches, Hindustan Lever is a subsidiary of British Unilever. It saw its profits soar after it started selling shampoo in single-serving packages (Prahalad 2005).

6 Recognising that this is a potentially large, new market, HP was involved in a microfinance project in Uganda, contributing to the development of a remote transaction system based on a cellular network.

7 This project was already under way at the time of the Seattle conference, and was presented there as a case study of 'digital dividends in action' (www.digitaldividend.org/about/about_01_confa.htm, accessed 13 January 2009).

When these did not materialise, e-Inclusion underwent a strategic reorientation in autumn 2001. The first generation of programme leaders were replaced with more business-oriented people.[8] The programme left Costa Rica for the larger markets of Brazil, India and South Africa and spun off an Emerging Markets Solutions (EMS) Group which was directly responsible for producing a return on HP's e-Inclusion investment. The main objective of EMS was to develop the programme's indirect and direct bop strategies.

Working at the bop

The indirect bop strategy—where e-Inclusion worked with public-sector organisations that had, until then, been marginal to the company's business—was most successfully executed in e-Inclusion's i-community in Mogalakwena, South Africa. i-communities were:

> communities where information and communication technology is strategically deployed for repeatable and sustainable socio-economic development. It provides HP with an emergent markets laboratory for development and piloting of solutions and business models. This new approach balances community values with business objectives and return on investment (Emerging Market Solutions, HP 2003, unpublished document).

i-communities' definition as 'inclusive communities' was reminiscent of Prahalad's 'inclusive capitalism' (Prahalad 2005). Mogalakwena followed e-Inclusion's first i-community in Kuppam in the Indian state of Andhra Pradesh.

The South African i-community was launched by President Thabo Mbeki during the United Nation's World Summit on Sustainable Development in Johannesburg in September 2002. HP was also the exclusive worldwide technology partner for the summit, which not only represented a large contract but also earned the company praise from national leaders in front of a worldwide audience. An e-Inclusion promotional video captured Mbeki recounting that when he was checking the preparedness of each venue before the summit, he saw HP computers everywhere. 'That's the first time I realised how big [HP's] contribution was. Thank you Carly and HP, it's been critical to ensuring the success that everybody is talking about.' Entering such a high-profile partnership with the United Nations thus brought worldwide publicity for HP, e-Inclusion and the Mogalakwena i-community. As a result, HP was earning 'goodwill translating into additional business' from governments and other development organisations (Emerging Market Solutions, HP 2003, unpublished document: 11).

In South Africa,

> the recognition given to the i-community work by President Thabo Mbeki has positioned the project to have dedicated national, provincial and municipal dollars assigned to it. In Q4 2003 this work was instrumental in the South Africa business team winning a Telkom deal worth $106 million (Emerging Market Solutions, HP 2003, unpublished document: 13).

HP was using its e-Inclusion work to make itself known, as a responsible company, to multilateral development organisations and developing countries' governments, and was succeeding in translating that recognition into public contracts (Engardio and Smith 2001).[9]

---

8 There were also macro-economic factors causing e-Inclusion's reorientation, such as the bursting of the dot-com bubble, the events of September 11 and the subsequent slump in the US economy, and the announcement of the Compaq merger.

9 Working with governments can also backfire, as happened in Kuppam, where the main champion of HP's i-community, Andhra Pradesh's Chief Minister Chandrababu Naidu, was voted out of office in 2004, with negative effects on HP's work in Kuppam (Braund *et al.* 2007).

In sum, the company's indirect bop strategy resulted from the realisation that support from large public-sector organisations was crucial for the success of e-Inclusion, both in terms of increased business for the company and of the economic sustainability and impact of e-Inclusion. It was through these organisations that e-Inclusion wanted to channel the benefits of its technologies to the poor.[10] As a culmination of these efforts, in early 2004 HP established a global public-sector organisation in addition to its three organisations targeting consumers, enterprise and the small and medium businesses segments.

e-Inclusion's direct bop strategy was executed through a number of pilot projects that aimed to develop and test new bop products, services and business models using HP's mobile technologies, while creating novel sources of income for the rural poor. In Costa Rica, the Digital Broker project sent young people door-to-door with PDAs (handheld computers), selling Internet services such as email, searches, printouts, photos and web design to housewives, students and small businesses. The brokers then went to the LINCOS container to fill the orders, for which they charged a small fee. This fee was split between the brokers and the container, and, together with a small HP salary, the brokers were able to make a modest living. The service was well received and used locally, and also judged to have been a success by HP's project manager, since it made the HP brand known throughout the community and provided market data about rural Internet consumption (Bossinger 2002). A similar project was developed in India around laptop computers, where so-called computer literacy professionals (CLPs) went door to door and provided e-services, ranging from health information to emails.

In another Indian pilot, the company trained rural women as village photographers, who took pictures with HP digital cameras, then printed them on the spot on printers hooked up to solar panels. Each village photographer was given her own suitcase that contained the equipment, and once again travelled door to door, or field to field, offering her services for a small fee. HP's goal in this project was to develop a bop alternative to its US$30,000 digital photographer studio. The company also wanted to gather information about the use of photography by the rural poor. Project managers were surprised to learn that the women took pictures of dead livestock when proof had to be submitted to an insurance company, of people participating in public works projects to support claims for two bags of rice, and of calendar images of gods for people who could not afford the original. Once again the project was judged to have been successful by all involved (Schwittay 2008).

The termination of all three projects by HP, in ways that left local participants disappointed and frustrated, reveals the power differentials between a multinational, multi-billion-dollar company and rural inhabitants (Schwittay 2008). Ensuring that people do not feel used by companies 'as guinea pigs', as one of the CLPs put it, in corporate 'living labs' (Dunn and Yamashita 2003) is the first lesson to be learned from e-Inclusion, and other corporate citizenship projects that work directly with marginalised groups (Schwittay 2008). In the second part of this paper I will present additional lessons from e-Inclusion, and their application to current corporate citizenship flagship programmes in the IT industry.

---

10 In Mogalakwena, e-Inclusion's accomplishments included an online portal in three local languages, community technology access centres and technology skills training centres, among others.

Learning from e-Inclusion

e-Inclusion was ended in the summer of 2005 because, as Fiorina's pet project, its termination was an easy way for her successor to distance himself from her. More importantly, the programme never delivered the social or business values to warrant its continued existence at a time of cost-cutting and corporate restructuring. Although nothing has taken e-Inclusion's place at HP, other high-tech companies have implemented their own flagship initiatives, which stand to benefit from e-Inclusion's lessons.

Intel's World Ahead

Intel's flagship programme—a billion-dollar initiative 'to connect the next billion people to uncompromised technology around the world'[11]—most closely approximates e-Inclusion's personal leadership style. Craig Barrett, Intel's Chairman, has assumed a high public profile as the Chair of the United Nations' Global Alliance for ICT and Development (UN-GAID).[12] In that position, he champions the efforts of the UN-GAID, commending its principles to foreign governments and trying to create action around its policy statements.[13] His global travels as both GAID and Intel chairman—from the village of Parintins in the Amazonian rainforest to the National Hospital in the Nigerian capital of Abuja to the Arab-Jewish Center in Haifa, Israel—can be followed on the World Ahead website. Closer to home, in February 2007 Intel hosted the UN-GAID Strategy Council meeting at its headquarters, together with a day-long event on 'The UN Connecting with Silicon Valley'. Similar to the ways in which Fiorina had used the UN as a platform to showcase HP's corporate citizenship work, so Barrett will rarely be seen without a piece of Intel technology, most prominently Intel's Classmate PC.

The danger of such a personalisation is that, when the champion leaves, no matter what the circumstances, the programme might suffer. However, World Ahead is tied closely to Intel's long-standing commitment to education, and especially teacher training. This not only assures programme support beyond its personal figurehead, but also provides focus and helps to integrate this corporate citizenship activity with Intel's mainstream businesses.

The lack of such integration was one of the shortcomings of the Kuppam i-community, as acknowledged by Dunn: 'we were not as successful in aligning the project with HP's business organisation in India so they never really felt a sense of ownership' (quoted in Braund *et al.* 2007: 31). This was in spite of the fact that HP Labs Bangalore had opened shortly after the i-community was set up with the explicit objective of supporting the project (HP 2001).[14]

Employee ownership of corporate citizenship programmes can not only contribute to their sustainability, but can also motivate employees in return.

IBM's Corporate Service Corps

One of the perceived benefits of corporate citizenship work is employee attraction, motivation and retention (Backhaus *et al.* 2004; Peterson 2004). During the dark days of the Compaq merger at HP, disillusioned employees would sometimes come to one partic-

---

11 www.intel.com/intel/worldahead, accessed 13 January 2009.
12 The UN-GAID is the successor of the UN's ICT Taskforce, which was instituted under Kofi Annan. Fiorina shared a seat with John Chambers, CEO of Cisco Systems on its Advisory Board.
13 This is not without risk in the traditionally UN-averse world of Silicon Valley (RiOS Institute 2007).
14 In the beginning, the i-community was managed by a Bangalore employee, who made the four-hour round trip to Kuppam a couple of times a month (Schwittay 2008).

ularly passionate e-Inclusion manager to be inspired by his work stories and his belief in the greatness of HP. However, when the same employee realised that upper management was not genuinely committed to creating social benefits through the programme and instead was just 'messing with other people's lives', he became a very cynical and disappointed 'warm body'—a far cry from the committed workforce corporate citizenship programmes are said to create.

In addition, passion and good intentions alone are not enough to make a successful 'corporate broker' between the company and community organisations (Buhl 1996). Employees need a combination of management expertise, international development experience and technical capabilities, and some companies have set up programmes to provide these skills. One example is IBM's Corporate Service Corps, which was established in 2007 with the objective to 'develop leadership skills while addressing socioeconomic challenges in key strategic emerging markets' (Thompson 2008).[15]

This programme is placing 600 IBM employees with non-governmental organisations (NGOs) that use technology for development purposes in six different countries (*News and Observer* 2008). There were 5,000 applicants for the first 100 jobs, which came complete with language and cultural training and then sent employees for four weeks to Romania, Turkey, Vietnam, the Philippines, Ghana and Tanzania. IBM hopes to give its employees 'real-world training' and 'a street view of emerging-market business problems', as well as 'a more culturally immersed experience' (*News and Observer* 2008). This makes the Corporate Service Corps the equivalent of the technology Peace Corps which, according to Prahalad, will give corporate executives a better understanding of emerging-market dynamics (Prahalad 2005).

AMD's 50x15

One objective of giving employees such on-the-ground exposure is to ensure that the products, services or solutions that will be developed and marketed under their leadership will be appropriate to the bop. Evidence that such appropriateness matters abounds, from computers that sit unused because the local electricity supply is unreliable to solar panels turned into tables to mountains of equipment succumbed to heat and wind exposure (Brewer *et al.* 2006). In fact, e-Inclusion's first project—the LINCOS recycled shipping container—is a good example of the failure to make ICTs, and the ways in which they are locally installed, meaningful and relevant. This in turn contributed directly to the lack of local ownership of the project and ultimately its demise (Granqvist 2005; Braund and Schwittay 2006). One way to avoid such a disconnect is to partner with local organisations and to pay special attention to issues of design, which AMD is doing in its flagship corporate citizenship programme.

Entitled 50x15, this programme aims to connect 50% of the world's population to the Internet by 2015.[16] It has been able to build a large ecosystem of local partners around the world. Some of these partnerships are unique, such as the programme's collaboration with Architects for Humanity (AFH), a non-profit organisation based in Sausalito, California, which uses architecture and design to bring about social change. 50x15 and AFH teamed up to launch an open design competition, and AMD awarded US$250,000 for the design and construction of a site-specific technology access centre in the developing world. The winner, Global Studio of Seattle, was announced in June 2008, and will build a technology media lab and recording studio in Mukuru Kwa Njenga, an informal settlement of 250,000 people in Nairobi, Kenya. Global Studio will be working with

---

15 The Service Corps is part of the Global Citizen's portfolio initiative announced by IBM's CEO Sam Palmisano in 2007.

16 www.50x15.com, accessed 13 January 2009.

a local organisation, whose founders hope that with the technology centre their community will become 'the next Silicon Valley'.[17] There were also regional winners, and some of the designs submitted for the competition will be used to develop future 50x15 Learning Labs, which provide the physical infrastructure for AMD's programme.

Another way to ensure appropriate technology design and implementation is to conduct more up-front and on-the-ground research that will inform the development process, as is done by Microsoft Research India.

Microsoft Research India

This R&D unit in Bangalore, India, counts among its staff not only software designers and computer scientists, but also sociologists and anthropologists. They are encouraged to conduct ethnographic research in rural sites, in order to get a better understanding of local needs and conditions. One of the results of this process was the development of a decidedly non-software programme called 'Farmer Idol', where local farmers star in videotaped spots providing farming training and tips that are distributed to their peers on DVDs (Vance 2008). The programme has been so successful that it will be spun off as an independent non-profit organisation.

e-Inclusion had attempted a similar learning process when its employees conducted 'immersion exercises' of living with Kuppam families for a couple of days (Emerging Market Solutions, HP 2003, unpublished document). The knowledge that was gained was limited, however, by the short amount of time and the narrow objective of the i-community to use HP technologies to solve what were essentially social and political problems (Schwittay 2008). In contrast to such corporate market research, academic research is less circumscribed by desired outcomes and can yield more relevant and useful information.

Microsoft Research India is encouraging such open-ended research among its employees. It is also actively shaping the academic discourse around what has become known as ICTD (information and communication technology and development) by sponsoring the foremost academic conference on the subject. The third instalment of that conference, ICTD 2009, will take place in Doha, Qatar, in April 2009, and Bill Gates is the confirmed keynote speaker. This will give him another opportunity to talk about 'creative capitalism' and how ICT can contribute to making the world a more equitable place. He will thereby continue a discussion he started almost a decade earlier at the Creating Digital Dividend conference.

Conclusion

In his closing keynote address at the Seattle event, Gates told his audience that the poor most likely need food, clean water and access to medicine before computers will be of use to them. In spite of this caution, high-tech leaders, among them Microsoft, have developed a number of global corporate citizenship initiatives to bring ICTs to unconnected people and places at the bop, thereby also providing them with access to information and electronic services.

C.K. Prahalad's ideas remain the guiding light of these programmes, which are driven by the search for emerging markets, as well as knowledge about them and products

---

17 50x15.amd.com/en-us/news_feature_item.aspx?iid=106, accessed 13 January 2009.

and services affordable and appropriate for them. However, as Bruno Lavin, a World Bank economist, has pointed out:

> The arithmetic of telecommunications and that of poverty do not necessarily seem to agree. For a poverty fighter, the 'next billion' would refer to those who need to be taken out of absolute poverty; for an IT executive, the 'next billion' would more spontaneously refer to the next wave of customers that could emerge from developing countries, particularly in the mobile market (Lavin 2005: 15).

All the programmes presented here are aiming more at the 'next billion' rather than the 'bottom billion', and the gap between the two groups must be acknowledged if corporate citizenship programmes in the high-tech industry are to be sustainable and bring about meaningful change. This is the most important legacy of e-Inclusion.

e-Inclusion was established by HP at a time when corporate citizenship was being embraced in earnest by corporate America, and also marks the beginning of strategic flagship digital divide initiatives in the IT industry. Its study can thus contribute much to our understanding of the emergence and evolution of corporate citizenship.

References

Anders, G. (2003) *Perfect Enough: Carly Fiorina and the Reinvention of Hewlett-Packard* (New York: Penguin).

Backhaus, K., B. Stone and K. Heiner (2004) 'Exploring the Relationship between Corporate Social Performance and Employer Attractiveness', *Business and Society* 41.3: 292-305.

Bossinger, S. (2002) 'The Information Broker Concept: An Innovative, Business-Driven Method of Delivering Information e-Services', unpublished white paper; 209.85.173.132/search?q=cache:heYn TztNj74J:members.tripod.com/societyarts/01sinf/wp/infobrokerwhitepaper.pdf+bossinger+scott+e-inclusion&hl=en&ct=clnk&cd=9&gl=us&client=firefox-a, accessed 22 January 2009.

Braund, P., and A. Schwittay (2006) 'The Missing Piece: The Importance of Human-Centered Research in ICTD', *ICTD 2006*, Berkeley, California, 25–26 May 2006.

——, K. Frauscher, D. Petkoski and A. Schwittay (2007) *ICT for Economic Development: Possibilities for Multisector Collaborations* (Washington, DC: World Bank Institute).

Brewer, E., M. Demmer, M. Ho, R.E. Honicky, J. Pal, M. Plauche and S. Surana (2006) 'The Challenges of Technology Research for Developing Regions', *IEEE Pervasive Computing* 5.2: 15-23.

Buhl, L. (1996) 'The Ethical Frame of Corporate Philanthropy', in D. Burlingame and D. Young (eds.), *Corporate Philanthropy at the Crossroads* (Bloomington, IN: Indiana University Press).

Burrows, P. (2003) *Backfire: Carly Fiorina's High-Stakes Battle for the Soul of Hewlett-Packard* (Hoboken, NJ: John Wiley).

Caudron, S. (2003) 'Don't Mess with Carly', *Workforce Management*, July 2003: 29-33.

Collins, J., and J. Porras (1994) *Built to Last: Successful Habits of Visionary Companies* (New York: Harper-Business).

Dunn, D., and K. Yamashita (2003) 'Microcapitalism and the Megacorporation', *Harvard Business Review*, August 2003: 47-54.

Engardio, P., and G. Smith (2001) 'Smart Globalization', *BusinessWeek*, 20–27 August 2001: 17.

Escobar, A. (1995) *Encountering Development: The Making and Unmaking of the Third World* (Princeton, NJ: Princeton University Press).

Fiorina, C. (2000) 'The Digital Ecosystem', speech delivered at the *World Resources Institute Conference: Creating Digital Dividends*, Seattle, WA, 16 October 2000; www.hp.com/hpinfo/execteam/speeches/fiorina/ceo_worldres_00.html, accessed 22 January 2009.

Granqvist, M. (2005) 'Looking Critically at ICT4Dev: The Case of Lincos', *Journal of Community Informatics* 2.1: 17-25.

Hart, S. (1997) 'Beyond Greening: Strategies for a Sustainable World', *Harvard Business Review*, January/February 1997: 67-76.

HP (2001) 'HP's Pioneering Approach to Social Venture Philanthropy Goes Global', HP press release 10/11/01; www.hp.com/hpinfo/newsroom/press/2001/011011a.html, accessed 22 January 2009.

Kirkpatrick, D. (2001) 'Great Leap Forward: Looking for Profits in Poverty', *Fortune* 2.5: 37.

Lavin, B. (2005) 'The Next Billion', *Communications and Strategies* 58: 15.

Malone, M. (2007) *Bill and Dave: How Hewlett and Packard Built the World's Greatest Company* (New York: Portfolio).

News and Observer (2008) 'Over There: Local tech companies establish beachheads in emerging markets', *News and Observer*, 11 May 2008; telecom-expense-management-solutions.tmcnet.com/news/2008/05/11/3438005.htm, accessed 13 January 2009.

Packard, D. (1995) *The HP Way: How Bill Hewlett and I Built Our Company* (New York: HarperBusiness).

Peterson, D. (2004) 'The Relationship between Perceptions of Corporate Citizenship and Organizational Commitment', *Business and Society* 43: 296-312.

Prahalad, C.K. (2005) *The Fortune at the Bottom of the Pyramid: Eradicating Poverty through Profit and Enabling Dignity and Choice through Markets* (Upper Saddle River, NJ: Wharton School Publications).

—— and A. Hammond (2002) 'Serving the World's Poor, Profitably', *Harvard Business Review*, September 2002: 48-57.

Rankin, K. (2001) 'Governing Development: Neoliberalism, Microcredit and Rational Economic Woman', *Economy and Society* 30.1: 18-37.

RiOS Institute (2007) *Building Common Ground: The UN Connecting with Silicon Valley* (New York: United Nations).

Schwittay, A. (2008) 'A Living Lab: Corporate Delivery of ICT in India', *Science, Technology and Society* 13.2: 175-209.

Smith, C.W. (2002) *Digital Corporate Citizenship: The Business Response to the Digital Divide* (Indianapolis, IN: The Center on Philanthropy at Indiana University).

Thompson, K. (2008) 'IBM Podcast with Janet Longmore'; www.dotrust.org/dot/www/who-we-are/news/ibm-podcast-with-janet-longmore, accessed 13 January 2009.

Vance, A. (2008) 'Microsoft goes far afield to study emerging markets', *New York Times*, 26 October 2008: B8.

Waugh, B. (2001) *The Soul in the Computer: The Story of a Corporate Revolutionary* (Maui, HI: Inner Ocean).

Willmott, M. (2001) *Citizen Brands: Putting Society at the Heart of your Business* (New York: John Wiley).

Book Review

Holger Backhaus-Maul, Christiane Biedermann, Stefan Nährlich and Judith Polterauer (eds.)
Corporate Citizenship in Deutschland:
Bilanz und Perspektiven
Wiesbaden: VS Verlag für Sozialwissenschaften, 2008, 541 pp paper

reviewed by Daniel Kinderman
Cornell University, USA

THERE ARE SEVERAL REASONS TO TAKE AN interest in the state of corporate citizenship (CC) in Germany, and in this book. On one hand, Germany is said by many to have 'lagged behind' on CC matters. (Sandra Waddock, Simon Zadek and others suggest CC is a set of collaborative values and institutional practices that govern government, business and NGO interactions in a shared problem domain). However, CC discourse and practice has encountered rapidly growing interest during recent years. What is going on? What accounts for this state of affairs? The volume *Corporate Citizenship in Deutschland*, edited by Holger Backhaus-Maul, Christiane Biedermann, Stefan Nährlich and Judith Polterauer, is a good place to look for answers to this question. It is the most comprehensive study of CC theory and practice in Germany published to date.

The book comprises six sections: (I) introduction, (II) social and economic debates, (III) empirical studies, (IV) strategies and instruments, (V) presentations of engaged companies and views on them from the media, and (VI) sociopolitical analyses and perspectives. It contains an unusually large number of contributions: over three dozen from scholars, entrepreneurs and managers, and journalists. While the essays by Jeremy Moon/Andy Crane/Dirk Matten, Thomas Beschorner, and Josef Wieland have been published previously, most are original. Collectively, they provide an overview of the heterogeneous state of corporate citizenship in Germany, and of debates associated with this emergent, paradoxical phenomenon.

Reading this book, one is struck by the breadth and diversity of views on corporate citizenship in Germany. Indeed, the authors have very different understandings about the descriptive state of affairs of CC in Germany and perhaps equally divergent views of its normative basis. The book seems intended both for those who want to understand and explain the empirical dynamics of corporate citizenship in Germany in comparison with other countries, and for those who are committed to advancing the corporate citizenship agenda.

There is nothing per se objectionable about this mix—though at times this reviewer wished that the argumentation had been pursued in a more sustained way across the contributors' essays. Despite this caveat, the authors contribute in original and stimulating ways to our understanding of CC in Germany and more generally.

Space constraints prevent me from describing all of the volume's essays; my account is necessarily selective. In their introduction, the editors set the stage for the volume. They do a good job of identifying the major issues and weaving together the heterogeneous fabric of the volume. Anja Schwerk probes the relationship between CC and corporate governance. Judith Polterauer surveys existing literature and makes a plausible case for what should and what should not be counted as corporate citizenship. She defines CC engagement as 'the voluntary, not-for-profit, continuous engagement of private sector firms in ways that go beyond the firms' core business activities but is simultaneously closely related to them' (p. 152; my translation). Polterauer's exercise is useful given the amorphousness of the term. Jörn Lamla draws on Luc Boltanski and Eve Chiapello's *New Spirit of Capitalism* to inquire about the potential of consumerist or artistic critique to further social and environmental ends.

Julia Egbringhoff and Gerd Mutz assess the relationship between works councils and CC initiatives. They find that works councils and CC are often like ships passing in the night: CC is often conducted without the knowledge or involvement of works councils. Given this lack of engagement, they conclude that CC has an ambivalent, if not contradictory, quality from the perspective of employees' representatives. Henry Schäfer investigates the function of rating agencies in furthering the cause of CC. Rudolf Speth argues that CC and lobbying have much in common. Frank Heuberger makes a case for the importance of communicative rationality (*à la* Jürgen Habermas) for the development of corporate citizenship.

Viewing the volume as a whole, it seems that the authors have very different understandings of the empirical state of affairs of corporate citizenship in Germany as well as the state of affairs that is normatively desirable. This could be seen as a weakness insofar as some of the essays are at tension and even at cross purposes with others, and because they do not aim towards the advancement of a single unified and coherent research agenda. This is not to deny the achievement of bringing together a wide spectrum of quality contributions in a single volume. The volume's heterogeneity can also be viewed as a strength, since its diverse contributions elucidate different empirical and theoretical facets of CC, and the contrasting arguments and interpretations reflect real tensions, paradoxes and ambivalences in the understanding and practice of corporate citizenship in Germany today.

One of these tensions concerns the relationship between CC and the transformations of German capitalism during the past decade. In their introduction, the editors observe that

> on the whole, the Corporate Citizenship discussion about the new role of firms in society is evolving relatively late and remarkably sluggishly, despite—or maybe precisely because—companies in Germany can look back on a decades-long tradition of engagement in the tradition of the national welfare state (p. 33)

Social partnership and some of the egalitarian and redistributive functions of the German social market economy model are eroding as the state offloads social responsibilities onto society. This, the editors note, is the context in which CC has gained prominence in Germany. But what role does CC fulfil in this transformation? The answers to this question vary in the volume. A number of contributors see CC as a positive-sum cooperative enterprise between business and civil society that addresses societal challenges and intractable social problems without itself affecting the balance between business, the state and civil society. For example, André Habisch writes that 'as part of civil society socially engaged firms neither can nor want to replace state activities' (p. 110). By contrast, other contributors endorse CC while stressing the necessity of unburdening business from institutionalised social responsibilities, such as taxation and social insurance contributions, as a *quid pro quo* for their increased engagement. They clearly imply that the state should do less as responsible corporate citizens do more.

The editors and contributors could have done more to draw out, reflect on and theorise this tension. Could it be that there is not only a correlation, but also a causal link between the rise of corporate citizenship in Germany during the past decade, and the transformation of the German economy, by which I mean the erosion of the 'German Model' or 'Rhenish' social market economy during the same period? I have argued something along these lines, setting the rise of CC in the context of the simultaneous decline and dismantling of 'organised capitalism' and institutionalised solidarity in Germany.[1]

The failure of the volume as a whole to develop a sustained, overarching and systematic argument is a weakness, but this shortcoming must be balanced against the thoughtfulness and generally high quality of the individual contributions and the identification of fruitful lines for further inquiry. While there is room to quibble—for example, it is not clear why the CC organisation UPJ, which has been among the 'pioneers' of CC in Germany since its founding in the mid-1990s, was not included—I recommend this book to everyone with a reading knowledge of German and an interest in corporate citizenship in Germany.

✉ Daniel Kinderman, Government Department, 214 White Hall, Cornell University, Ithaca, NY, 14853-4601 USA

🖥 dpk24@cornell.edu

---

1 Daniel Kinderman, 'The Political Economy of Corporate Responsibility in Germany, 1995–2008', Working Paper 5, Germany in Global Economic Governance Series, Mario Einaudi Center for International Studies, Cornell University, 2008; www.einaudi.cornell.edu/initiatives/working.asp?view=44.

About the Journal of Corporate Citizenship

THE JOURNAL OF CORPORATE CITIZENSHIP (JCC) is a multidisciplinary peer-reviewed journal that focuses on integrating theory about corporate citizenship with management practice. It provides a forum in which the tensions and practical realities of making corporate citizenship real can be addressed in a reader-friendly, yet conceptually and empirically rigorous format.

JCC aims to publish *the best ideas integrating the theory and practice of corporate citizenship in a format that is readable, accessible, engaging, interesting and useful* for readers in its already wide audience in business, consultancy, government, NGOs and academia. It encourages practical, theoretically sound, and (when relevant) empirically rigorous manuscripts that address real-world implications of corporate citizenship in global and local contexts. Topics related to corporate citizenship can include (but are not limited to): corporate responsibility, stakeholder relationships, public policy, sustainability and environment, human and labour rights/issues, governance, accountability and transparency, globalisation, small and medium-sized enterprises (SMEs) as well as multinational firms, ethics, measurement, and specific issues related to corporate citizenship, such as diversity, poverty, education, information, trust, supply chain management, and problematic or constructive corporate/human behaviours and practices.

In addition to articles linking the theory and practice of corporate citizenship, JCC also encourages innovative or creative submissions (for peer review). Innovative submissions can highlight issues of corporate citizenship from a critical perspective, enhance practical or conceptual understanding of corporate citizenship, or provide new insights or alternative perspectives on the realities of corporate citizenship in today's world. Innovative submissions might include: critical perspectives and controversies, photography, essays, poetry, drama, reflections, and other innovations that help bring corporate citizenship to life for management practitioners and academics alike.

JCC welcomes contributions from researchers and practitioners involved in any of the areas mentioned above. Manuscripts should be written so that they are comprehensible to an intelligent reader, avoiding jargon, formulas and extensive methodological treatises wherever possible. They should use examples and illustrations to highlight the ideas, concepts and practical implications of the ideas being presented. Theory is important and necessary; but theory—with the empirical research and conceptual work that supports theory—needs to be balanced by integration into practices to stand the tests of time and usefulness. JCC aims to be the premier journal to publish articles on corporate citizenship that accomplish this integration of theory and practice. We want the journal to be read as much by executives leading corporate citizenship as it is by academics seeking sound research and scholarship.

JCC appears quarterly and the contents of each issue include: editorials; peer-reviewed papers by leading writers; a global digest of key initiatives and developments from the previous quarter; reviews; case studies; think-pieces; and an agenda of conferences and meetings. A key feature is the 'Turning Points' section. Turning Points are commentaries, controversies, new ideas, essays and insights that aim to be provocative and engaging, raise the important issues of the day and provide observations on what is too new yet to be the subject of empirical and theoretical studies. JCC continues to produce occasional issues dedicated to a single theme. These have included 'Is Corporate Citizenship Making a Difference?', 'The Corporate Contribution to One Planet Living in Global Peace and Security', 'Corporate Social Responsibility in Emerging Economies', 'Corporate Citizenship in Latin America' and 'Corporate Citizenship in Africa'.

EDITOR

General Editors: David Cooperrider and Ronald Fry, The Fowler Center for Sustainable Value, Weatherhead School of Management, Case Western Reserve University, USA; email: David.Cooperrider@case.edu and Ronald.Fry@case.edu.

Regional Editors:

North American Editor: Sandra Waddock, Professor of Management, Boston College, Carroll School of Management, Senior Research Fellow, Center for Corporate Citizenship, Chestnut Hill, MA 02467 USA; tel: +1 617 552 0477; fax: +1 617 552 0433; email: waddock@bc.edu

Australasia Editor: David Birch, Director, Corporate Citizenship Research Unit, Deakin University, 221 Burwood Highway, Melbourne, Victoria, Australia 3125; email: edjcc@bc.edu.

Asia-Pacific Editor: Malcolm McIntosh, Asia-Pacific Centre for Sustainable Enterprise, Griffith Business School, Australia; email: malcolm.mcintosh@btinternet.com.

Notes for Contributors

Submissions
Submissions via email (edjcc@bc.edu) are preferred if saved as Microsoft Word or RTF documents. Alternatively, two copies of the paper and a PC-compatible disk should be sent to: *Journal of Corporate Citizenship* Editorial Office, Boston College Center for Corporate Citizenship, Carroll School of Management, Chestnut Hill, MA 02467, USA; tel: +1 617 552 0477; fax: +1 617 552 0433; email: edjcc@bc.edu. Hard copies of all figures and tables will be required if the paper is accepted.

Presentation
Articles should be 4,000–6,000 words long. Manuscripts should be arranged in the following order of presentation.

First page: Title, subtitle (if any), author's name, affiliation, full postal address and telephone, fax and email. Respective affiliations, addresses and emails of co-authors should be clearly indicated. Please also include approximately 50 words of biographical information on all authors, and a good-quality photograph of each (digital files should be at least 300 dpi × 3 cm; otherwise include a print [not transparency]).

Second page: A self-contained abstract of up to 150 words summarising the paper and its conclusions; and between 7 and 10 keywords, which will reflect the core themes of the paper (anticipating possible search terms that might be used by a potential reader).

Subsequent pages: Main body of text; footnotes/endnotes; list of references; appendices; tables; illustrations.

Authors are urged to write as concisely as possible, but not at the expense of clarity. The main title of the article should be kept short, up to 40 characters including spaces, but may be accompanied by a subtitle if further clarification is desired. Descriptive or explanatory passages, intrinsically necessary but which tend to break the flow of the main text, should be expressed as footnotes or appendices.

References
All bibliographic references must be complete, comprising: authors and initials, full title and subtitle, place of publication, publisher, date, and page references. References to journal articles must include the volume and number of the journal and page extent. The layout should adhere to the following convention:

Clifton, R., and N. Buss (1992) 'Greener Communications', in M. Charter (ed.), *Greener Marketing: A Responsible Approach to Business* (Sheffield, UK: Greenleaf Publishing): 241-53.

Porter, M.E., and C. van der Linde (1995) 'Green and Competitive: Ending the Stalemate', *Harvard Business Review* 73.5 (September/October 1995): 120-33.

WCED (World Commission on Environment and Development) (1987) *Our Common Future* ('The Brundtland Report'; Oxford, UK: Oxford University Press).

These should be listed, alphabetically by author surname, at the end of the article. When citing, please use the 'author–date' method in parentheses, e.g. '(Ditz *et al.* 1995: 107)'.

Endnotes/Footnotes
Endnotes/footnotes should be numbered consecutively in Arabic numerals and placed at the end of the manuscript before any figures. Automatic endnotes/footnotes are acceptable if using Microsoft Word.

Tables, Graphs, etc.
All tables, graphs, diagrams and other drawings should be clearly referred to and numbered consecutively in Arabic numerals. Their position should be indicated in the text. All figures must have captions. In all figures taken or adapted from other sources, a brief note to that effect is obligatory, below the caption.

Photographs
Photographic material relevant to the article is encouraged and should be supplied at approx. 300 dpi × 7 cm, or as prints (not transparencies).

Copyright
Before publication, authors are requested to assign copyright to Greenleaf Publishing. This allows Greenleaf Publishing to sanction reprints and photocopies and to authorise the reprint of complete issues or volumes according to demand. Authors' traditional rights will not be jeopardised by assigning copyright in this manner, as they will retain the right to re-use.

Proofs
Authors are responsible for ensuring that all manuscripts (whether original or revised) are accurately typed before final submission. One set of proofs will be sent to authors before publication, which must be returned promptly.

▶ **To discuss ideas for contributions**, please contact the General Editors: David Cooperrider and Ronald Fry, The Fowler Center for Sustainable Value, Weatherhead School of Management, Case Western Reserve University, The Peter B. Lewis Building, 11119 Bellflower Road, Cleveland, OH 44106-7235, USA; emails: David.Cooperrider@case.edu and Ronald.Fry@case.edu.

For Product Safety Concerns and Information please contact our EU
representative GPSR@taylorandfrancis.com Taylor & Francis Verlag GmbH,
Kaufingerstraße 24, 80331 München, Germany

Printed and bound by CPI Group (UK) Ltd, Croydon, CR0 4YY

01/05/2025

01858399-0004